EASY-TO-MAKE WOODEN FURNITURE FOR CHILDREN

Paul Howard

John Murray

First published in Great Britain 1982 by
John Murray (Publishers) Ltd.,
50 Albemarle Street, London W1X 4BD
by arrangement with Personal Library, Publishers

Printed in Hong Kong by Wing King Tong Co. Ltd.

0 7195 3988 9

Acknowledgements

In considering who contributed most to my writing this book and making all the items featured, I think first of my daughter Penny.

She played with great enthusiasm with the items that were right for her, and ignored those that did not suit her. Whenever she heard me carrying anything up the basement stairs, she ran to greet me, exclaiming with delight as an article of furniture or toy was given to her. It was through her use of the things I built that I was able to modify and perfect the toys and furniture in this book.

The articles are now getting second use by her baby brother Peter. I am sure he has benefited and will continue to do so from her experiences.

Special thanks to the children in the photographs: Penny and Peter, Jake Mitchell, and Aaron and Meredith Woodley.

The dresses for Penny and Meredith were designed and made by Denise Woodley of York County Dress Works Inc., Toronto.

Contents

Part I / Introduction

Rearing a child can be an awesome experience. When I began to work on this book I had just become a first-time parent. I had two good reasons for deciding to make Penny's furniture and toys: one was economic, and the other, pleasure. Because my wife, Fiona, and I were saving to buy a boat, we did not have a lot of spare cash; and I enjoy working with my hands.

Designing and making the paraphernalia a child requires is a rewarding pastime. I found it was not difficult to be a do-it-yourself parent. The articles in this book have been designed and built by me, and have been baby-tested. Intended for the use of infants, toddlers and preschoolers, they are of simple construction with the clearest plans I could devise, and are suitable for the novice carpenter.

A total of thirty different projects are featured in the book, arranged approximately in the order you will need them. They are all relatively simple, but some good starter pieces for a first-time carpenter are baby's first cradle, the changing unit and the toy box. The most complicated pieces are the "jail bars" standard crib and the bunk beds.

NEED

One of the most difficult things to decide, especially for the first-time parent, is, what does one need? Right from the birth of the child we are bombarded with all kinds of advertising, books and brochures. The deluge starts with the hospital giveaway packets, and I doubt if it ever stops.

However, there does seem to be a consensus among learning-and-development specialists that children's things should be kept basic, simple and few. I am sure we have all witnessed the scene of a well-meaning relative giving an infant an expensive and elaborate present, only to have the child prefer to play with the wrapping paper and ribbon.

As the child grows older and the toys become even more elaborate, batteries run down and the plastic breaks, while wooden blocks continue to be stacked and anything that can be pushed or pulled remains a popular plaything. After the child graduates from crinkling paper, he still enjoys using paper—only now with paints and crayons. A full toy box does not necessarily mean a happy child.

Children love furniture that is scaled to their size and needs. An infant wants small things he can handle, mouth and rattle. A two-year-old prefers using his own table and stool to working on an adult-size table and chair.

CHILD DEVELOPMENT

A child's job is to explore and learn about the world around him, and adults often mislabel this work as "play." A child learns at his own pace. He will only be frustrated if confronted with things too large to manipulate or too difficult to master.

Up to six months the child stays more or less where he is put. He plays in his crib with objects dangling above or beside him, learning to recognize faces and textures as well as general sights and sounds. Mobiles, rattles, bells and stuffed animals are all interesting to an infant. He becomes a great watcher of movement around him: put his cradle in the living room during playtime, or lay him on the floor in the middle of the action in the home, and he will be well entertained.

An infant enjoys bright colors. Red, orange and yellow are best. Hang mobiles within 10 in. *(254 mm)* of his face so that he can reach out to touch and rattle them. Faces with large bright eyes are good for mobiles. Alternate the colors, shapes and expressions.

Research has shown that a newborn's vision begins to develop in seeing things from side to side, with up-and-down movement developing later. The newborn also prefers curved lines to straight, patterns to plain, and large simple designs to small ones.

By three to four months the child begins to roll around and tries to sit up. An infant crawler gives him early mobility by allowing him to push himself around before he is able to hold up his body and drag himself around.

By six months the child can sit up and thus gains a new perspective on the world. Prop him up in the middle of the room with a few pillows around him to cushion him when he topples over. Surround him with his toys and he will be content.

At this age the walker is good for him, since it again allows mobility besides keeping him upright. He strengthens his muscles for standing and walking while scooting around the room scattering his toys. Toys that can be pushed, rolled and picked up are his favorite, especially if they are colorful.

As the child's age nears one year he begins pulling himself to a standing position, although few children can walk before their first birthday. It is at this time that he tries to grasp everything within reach. He pulls things off the table toward himself and crawls under and into anything he can.

The toddler of one to two years loves objects he can push, especially if they help him to stand and walk. When he can walk well he will want to pull things. At this age a small gym with a place to crawl into is great fun.

At two years the child wants to become independent and craves activities that allow him self-expression. Scribbling and finger painting are messy but rewarding.

From two years to five years he needs a lot of vigorous play to fine-tune his skills of running, jumping, climbing and balancing. A large outdoor

BOYS
height

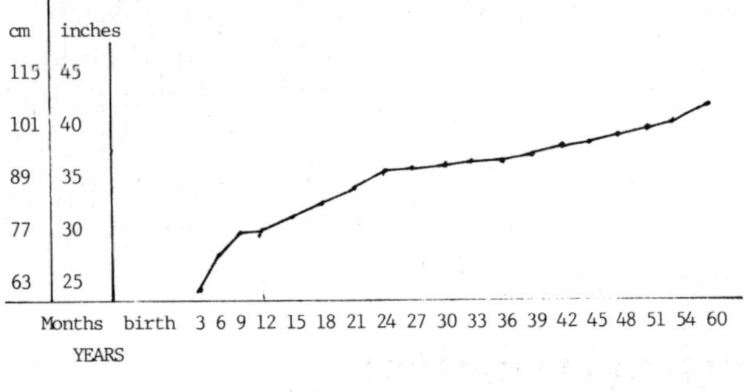

weight

Age (months)	birth	6	12	18	24	30	36	42	48	54	60
lbs.	8	17.6	23	26	28.6	31	33	35	37.5	39	41.5
Kilos	3.8	8	10.2	12	13	14	15	15.8	17	18	18.9

GIRLS
height

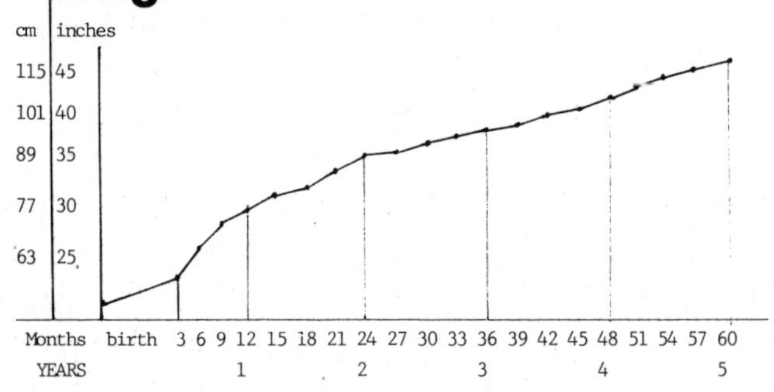

weight

Age (months)	birth	6	12	18	24	30	36	42	48	54	60
lbs.	7.5	15.5	20.5	24.5	26	30	32	34	36	38	40.5
kilos	3.4	7.2	9.5	11	12.2	13.2	14.2	15.2	16.2	17.2	18.2

gym and a swing would be fun, as well as a balancing bar or stilts. He becomes an accomplished artist with paint and crayons; now his drawings are more realistic, with faces, fingers, feet and other detailed work.

SIZES

The charts included show the approximate size and growth of the average child. Because the charts show a mythical average, your child's height and weight will not likely match the suggested figures at any given time. Regard the charts as only a rough guide to size and growth rate, and expect variations.

As an example, our daughter was born with a length of about 20 in. *(51 cm)* and weighed 7 lbs. 13 oz. *(3.6 kg)*. By consulting the chart you will see that she was slightly shorter, yet slightly heavier than average. Some friends of ours had a son a few months later who weighed 10 lb. *(4.8 kg)* at birth and was 24 in. *(61 cm)* long.

At six months Penny weighed 18 lb. *(8.2 kg)* and was 27 in. *(69 cm)* long. By this age she was slightly longer and heavier than average.

As the infant grows, his body proportions change. At birth a baby's head is approximately one-fourth of his total length, with his torso and legs each making up about three-eighths of his length. As he develops, his torso grows faster than the rest of his parts. By two years of age his head accounts for less than one-fourth of his length, with his torso making up the difference and his legs remaining at about the same proportion as at birth.

Body length and proportions are important when planning to custom-make furniture for your child. For instance, I show the first cradle as being 28½ in. *(72 cm)* long on the inside. An average child, or Penny, could sleep comfortably in this cradle until three to four months, as it was designed to be used. Our friend's child with a length of 24 in. *(61 cm)* at birth would soon be stretching his toes out and pushing his head against the end board. He would need a cradle somewhat longer.

As another example, a walker made for a larger-than-average child of about six months would have to be higher to accommodate his longer legs and torso. Measure your child as he grows and scale the plans according to his needs.

SAFETY

All parents are rightly concerned about their children's safety. Various government agencies in Canada and the United States concern themselves with the testing and regulation of toys and furniture for children.

In Canada the Hazardous Products Act outlines strict regulations for such things as cribs, cradles, paints and other surface coatings, toys and construction techniques.

Likewise in the U.S., the Consumer Products Safety Commission, through the Federal Hazardous Substances Act Regulations, establishes controls and testing procedures to ensure the safety of articles made for children.

The Canadian Toy Testing Council, a nonprofit organization, tests commercially available toys that are manufactured in Canada, the U.S. and other countries. This agency publishes an excellent guide to safe toys called Good Toys, listing the name, manufacturer, recommended age group and approximate price of more than five hundred toys, with comments. The booklet is updated regularly as new products on the market are tested. The same organization also publishes brochures offering tips on selecting toys, general safety and other related topics.

The Consumer Product Safety Commission in the U.S. publishes the Banned Toys List. Although it is not intended to be an all-inclusive shopping guide, it contains useful information resulting from the commission's constant testing of toys on the market to ensure that hazardous children's products are not sold. General brochures about safety and selection of toys for various age groups are also available from this agency.

The above-mentioned organizations are concerned with commercially available toys. As a "do-it-yourselfer" you can make whatever you like, but these regulations provide a good guideline for you when constructing articles intended for children's use.

The Canadian Hazardous Products Act gives specific measurements for the construction of, among other things, cribs. For example, rails should be 26 in. *(66 cm)* from the top of the mattress, and sliding gates must be 9 in. *(23 cm)* higher than the mattress when lowered. The plans for the crib included in this book conform to those regulations.

SAFETY IN STRENGTH

Strongly built toys or furniture are safer than weak items that fall apart with constant, though probably normal, use. When I design, build and test an article for a child, I consider that if I can sit, stand or hang from it with my weight of 175 lb. *(79 kg)*, a child is unlikely to be able to break it. As an example of this, I can and sometimes do sit on the walker made for a six-month-old child. It does not creak or groan under my weight, and after months of proper use it has not shown any signs of weakness or wobbling.

Many of the designs are reminiscent of the type of items commercially available before the advent of universal plastic molding. To some eyes they are boxlike, but they are strong, durable and time-tested. Where ease of building method and strength were in conflict with elegance, I opted for simplicity. The items included here are meant first and foremost to be functional.

SAFE PAINTS

Until recently lead-based paints posed a hazard to children. Now the lead content of household paints is regulated in the U.S. and Canada. Both the Canadian and American product-safety acts include sections limiting the amount of lead in household paints to 0.50 percent by weight of the contained solids, including pigments, film solids and driers. These regulations relate to latex and alkyd paints and varnishes. In Canada other metals such as mercury (which is prohibited), antimony, arsenic, cadmium, selenium and barium are regulated when the paint is to be used specifically for children's toys.

Paints such as Simpson's exterior-interior oil-base high-gloss enamel are recommended on the label for children's toys and, I have been told, conform to government regulations. Paints not specified for use on children's articles, but acceptable for household use, may contain varying amounts of the above metals and chemicals, since they are regulated primarily for lead content. These household paints are considered to be safe for use on children's furniture.

This is not to say it is safe for a child to ingest any surface coating, no matter what it is regulated for, since eating paint chips of any description can hardly be considered healthy.

When choosing paints, be sure you are using a household paint or one recommended for children's toys. Some commercial and exterior paints still have a high lead content and are not subject to government regulations. At the paint store let the sales clerk know the intended use of the coating, and request a paint recommended for children's toys or furniture. There are a few types of paint that have this marked on the label; the clerk will probably suggest an alkyd interior paint, which is what I generally use.

For most painting I use semigloss alkyd interior paint: it is durable and easy to wipe clean. The low-sheen finish of the semigloss helps hide imperfections in home finishes. I use the oil-base high-gloss paint for painting on designs or painting faces, since the colors are bright and shiny.

Urethane varnish is good for indoor use, but do not use it on articles that will be left out in the sun; this varnish cracks and peels quickly upon exposure to intense sunlight. The standard exterior varnishes are longer lasting for outdoor use.

For items such as an outdoor gym, stilts, or anything that gets a lot of rough treatment, use an oil-based stain that is also a wood preservative. It has the advantage of not peeling as paint would, and if the wood begins to weather, simply apply another coat.

Part II Building Plans

1 Baby's First Cradle

This cradle has served us well for our two children. In addition, it has done yeoman's service as a doll bed and toy box.

It was the first article I built for our child and will perhaps be your first baby furniture project, too. Easily constructed with a few tools, it is inexpensive and very sturdy.

After Penny outgrew the cradle we loaned it to a five-year-old friend for a doll bed. It received hard treatment in her care, as she would often sit in it with her dolls. When our second child was about to be born, all it needed was a fresh coat of paint. I am sure the cradle will last for generations.

What You Need

TOOLS: tape measure, drill with ¾ in. *(18 mm)* wood bit, coping saw, saber saw or jigsaw, hammer

MATERIALS:

¾ in. *(18 mm)* softwood dowels
- ☐ eighteen 30 in. *(762 mm)*

¾ in. *(20 mm)* plywood
- ☐ two pieces 12 in. x 18 in. *(305 mm x 460 mm)*

1½ in. *(40 mm)* finishing nails

- ☐ wood glue

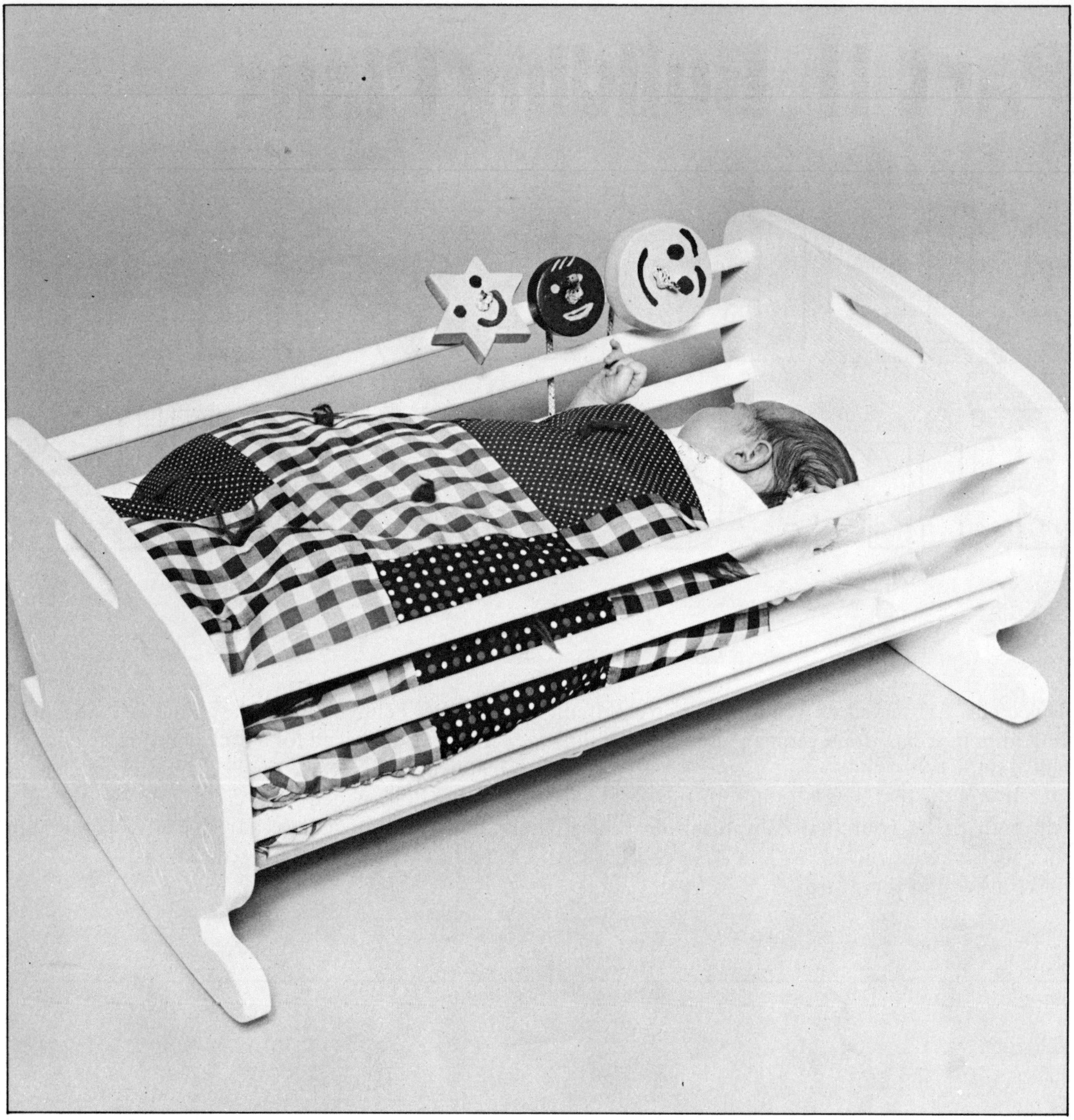

FIG. 1

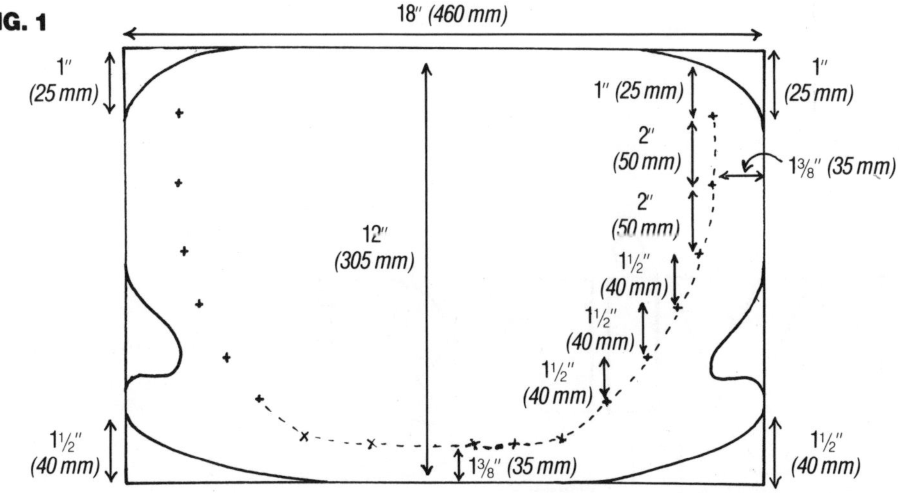

Building Instructions

Lay out the plywood ends as in **FIGURE 1**. If you do not want to make all the curved cuts, leave the ends rectangular or make any other shape. The rocker bottom is nice, and I like the shape that is shown.

For the rocker-bottom cradle, make a mark at the sides 1½ in. *(40 mm)* up from the corners, and another mark at the middle of the bottom edge. Use a flexible piece of thin wood or plastic to make the proper arc by bending it across these three points. Anything that will bend yet hold this shape, such as a ruler, stiff wire, tubing or aluminum molding, will work well as a marking guide. You will probably need someone to help hold it while you mark with the pencil.

As shown in **FIGURE 1**, make a pencil line around the end about 1⅜ in. *(35 mm)* from the edge, following the basic shape of the end piece. Mark the places where the holes for the dowels should be along this line. The top two dowels will be on 2 in. *(50 mm)* centers, with all the others on 1½ in. *(40 mm)* centers.

The dowels should fit quite snugly in the holes. Drill a test hole first in a scrap of wood; if the fit is loose you may have to file the drill slightly to decrease its diameter. See the section on dowels for instructions on how to do this.

When drilling the holes, drill only until the point comes through the wood, then turn the piece over and complete the drilling from the other side. This makes a much neater hole and facilitates your job of finishing.

When ready to assemble, with the dowels all cut to length, dab a bit of glue on a dowel end, then force it into the hole. Continue doing this until all of the dowels are started in one end.

Working quickly, before the glue sets, dab some glue around all of the other ends of the dowels and begin inserting them in the holes in the other end piece. This procedure may be a bit tedious, since some dowels will be fractionally longer than others, but get them all started and then force them through the holes until they are flush with the surface. Check the other end to be sure you did not pull some of the dowels partially out of the holes.

Lay the cradle on a flat surface and check to be sure there is no twist in it; the two end pieces should line up with each other both vertically and horizontally. If there is a slight twist, simply straighten it. When everything is straight, set a nail through from the edge of the plywood into each dowel at each end.

Sand and finish as desired.

2

Drying Rack

Collapsible racks have been used for a long time to dry small items. Make one to fit into a corner of your bathroom or bedroom for hanging out things that are damp or have just been rinsed. I made ours soon after the baby was born, and although it is collapsible for storing it has seen constant use since that time.

The drying rack is very easily put together; the project should take only a couple of hours from beginning to end. I did not put a finish on the wood, but left it bare. Sanding helps to reduce the splinters.

I used 1 in. x 2 in. *(17 mm x 38 mm)* spruce because it is less likely to split than fir or pine when working with such small pieces.

The length of the drying rack does not matter, since the dowels could be shorter or longer. If more than 36 in. *(1 m)* long, a ½ in. *(12 mm)* dowel might begin to sag when loaded: I would then use a larger dowel.

What You Need

TOOLS: saw, hammer, drill and ½ in. *(12 mm)* and ⅝ in. *(16 mm)* bit, measuring tape. *Optional:* miter box for cutting dowels and 1 in. x 2 in. *(17 mm x 38 mm)* file

MATERIALS: ½ in. *(12 mm)* softwood (cheaper) or hardwood dowels

- ☐ nine 30 in. *(762 mm)*
- ☐ two 27 in. *(685 mm)*

1 in. x 2 in. *(17 mm x 38 mm)* softwood (I used spruce)

- ☐ twelve pieces—21 in. *(533 mm)*
- ☐ two pieces—14 in. *(355 mm)*
- ☐ one piece—24½ in. *(622 mm)* to make fourteen—1¾ in. *(44 mm)* pieces
- ☐ 1¼ in. *(32 mm)* finishing nails

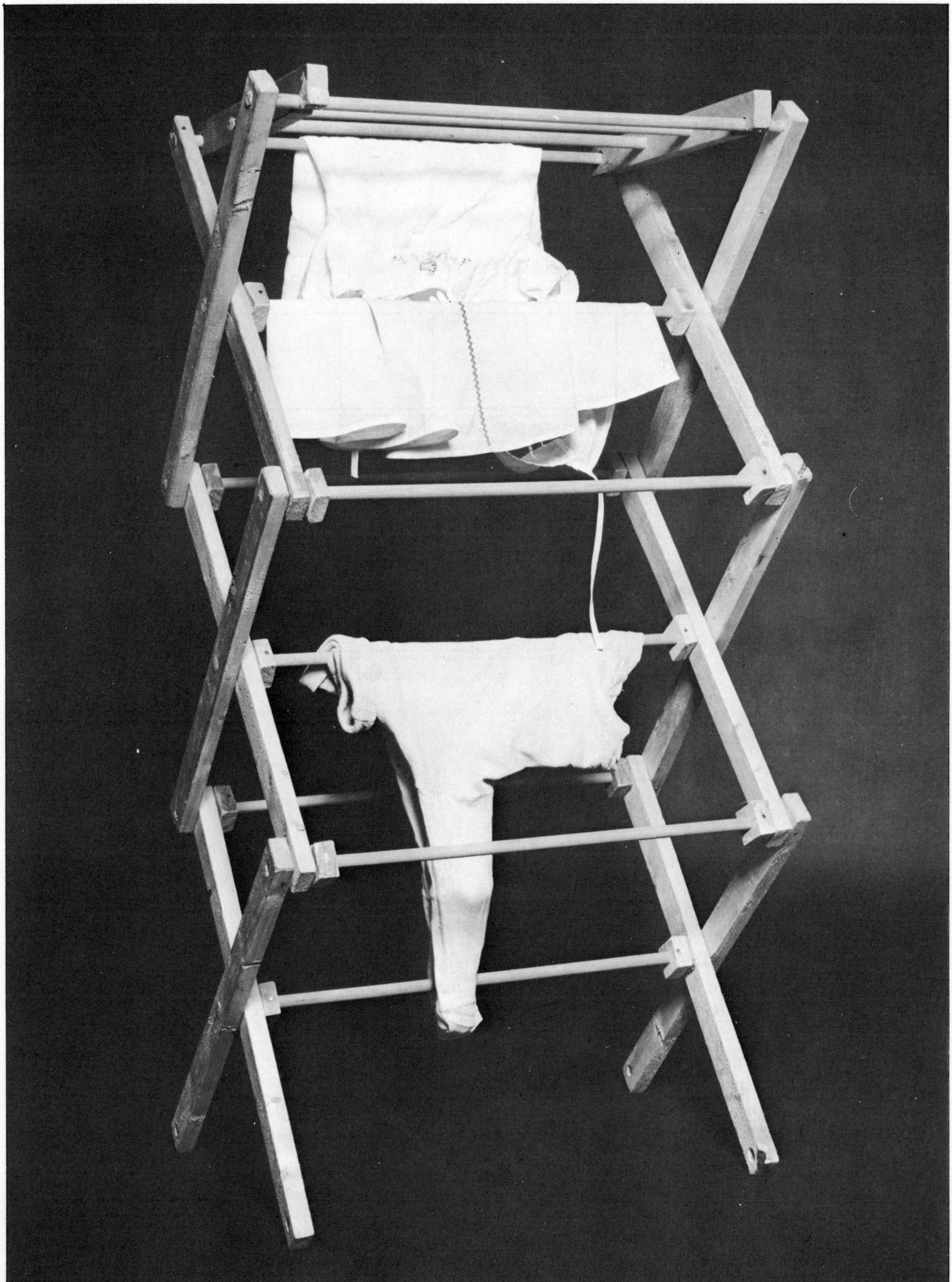

FIG. 1

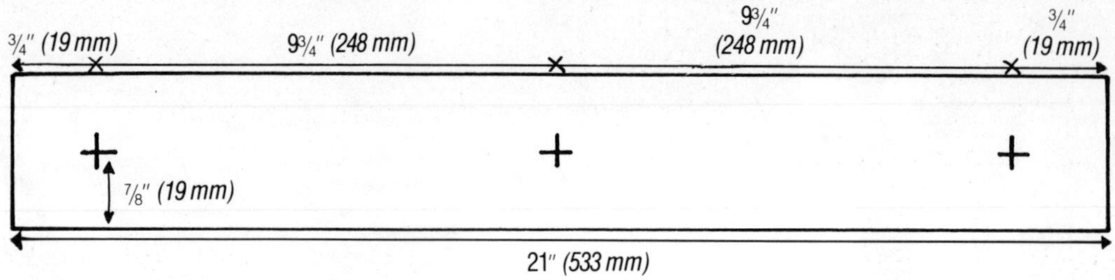

FIG. 2

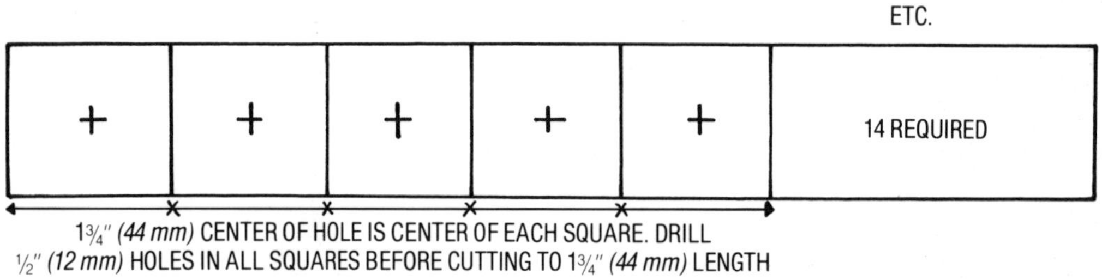

FIG. 3

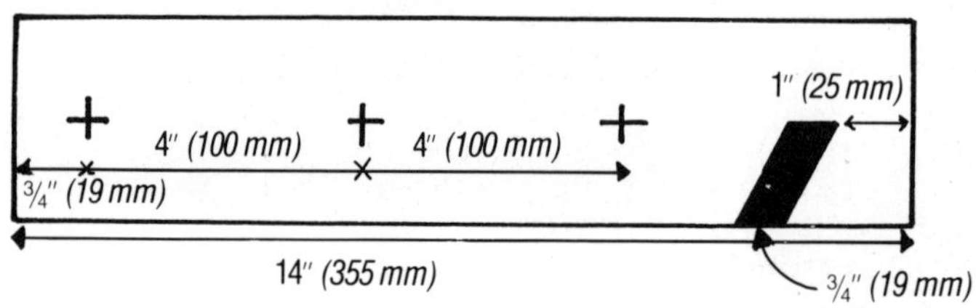

Building Instructions

Begin by cutting all the dowels and the 1 in. x 2 in. *(17 mm x 38 mm)* softwood to length, except for the fourteen 1¾ in. *(44 mm)* pieces. Although it is not necessary, a miter box can help to make the cuts straight on these small pieces.

With your electric drill and ⅝ in. *(16 mm)* wood-boring bit (a "spade" bit), drill holes near the ends and at the middle of four of the 1 in. x 2 in. *(17 mm x 38 mm)* pieces as in FIGURE 1. On two other 1 in. x 2 in. *(17 mm x 38 mm)* pieces, drill the hole in one end and the middle. The latter two will be the lower legs.

Use the ½ in. *(12 mm)* drill bit to make a hole in the wood in which the ½ in. *(12 mm)* dowel fits snugly. Make a trial hole in a scrap piece of wood: if the fit is loose, file the edges of the spade bit, both edges equally, until the dowel fits tightly into the hole.

Filing will not ruin the drill, since these inexpensive bits are cut quite inaccurately: in fact, the bit will be sharper after you are done. You will perhaps need to take off only 1/16 in. *(1 mm)*.

Use the ½ in. *(12 mm)* bit to drill the remaining six 1 in. x 2 in. *(17 mm x 38 mm)* pieces in the same manner as above, again leaving one end of two of the 1 in. x 2 in. *(17 mm x 38 mm)* undrilled.

Take the 1 in. x 2 in. *(17 mm x 38 mm)* softwood from which you will cut the fourteen 1¾ in. *(44 mm)* pieces and mark and drill as in FIGURE 2, using your ½ in. *(12 mm)* drill bit. When all the holes are drilled, cut these pieces to their 1¾ in. *(44 mm)* length.

The two 1 in. x 2 in. *(17 mm x 38 mm)* pieces that are 14 in. *(355 mm)* long should be cut and drilled as in FIGURE 3. Be careful when cutting the notch in the end, since the end could break off. If this does happen, nail and glue it back on, using one finishing nail and glue. If you still have problems, drill a hole and use a short piece of 3/8 in. *(9 mm)* or 1/4 in. *(6 mm)* dowel for the stopper.

Begin assembling the drying rack by sliding one of the 1 3/4 in. *(44 mm)* 1 in. x 2 in. *(17 mm x 38 mm)* pieces about 3 1/2 in. *(90 mm)* onto each end of all but two of the 30 in. *(762 mm)* dowels. Begin sliding onto the dowels one of the 1 in. x 2 in. *(17 mm x 38 mm)* pieces with the 5/8 in. *(16 mm)* holes and no hole at one end next to the short 1 in. x 2 in. *(17 mm x 38 mm)* pieces. Then fit a 1 in. x 2 in. *(17 mm x 38 mm)* with 1/2 in. *(12 mm)* holes at the outside.

Once started at the bottom of one side, just keep building it up. You will see from **FIGURES 4** and **5** how the rack is to be assembled. The two dowels without the 1 3/4 in. *(44 mm)* pieces are the top two dowels. The 14 in. *(355 mm)* 1 in. x 2 in. *(17 mm x 38 mm)* pieces will hinge on one of these and hook onto the other. The two 27 in. *(685 mm)* dowels belong in the holes in the latter two pieces.

When everything is assembled, turn the 1 3/4 in. *(44 mm)* pieces to align with the longer 1 in. x 2 in. *(17 mm x 38 mm)* when the rack is standing up. With the ends of the dowels flush with the outside of the 1 in. x 2 in. *(17 mm x 38 mm)*, push the short pieces next to the other, then put a nail through either edge that is not an end grain and into the dowel.

Also nail the outer 1 in. x 2 in. *(17 mm x 38 mm)*, the pieces with the 1/2 in. *(12 mm)* holes, to the dowels with one nail per end. *(Note: It is easier to drill a hole using a finishing nail with the head cut off as a drill and then push rather than pound the nails in place.)*

Nail the dowels that pass through the middle of the top piece—the two 27 in. *(685 mm)* in length—last, with the top 1 in. x 2 in. *(17 mm x 38 mm)* pushed as wide as possible.

When doing this nailing you may need someone to help hold the rack, and also to hold a piece of 2 in. x 4 in. *(38 mm x 89 mm)* or some other heavy object under the 1 in. x 2 in. *(17 mm x 38 mm)* as a backing piece while nailing.

FIG. 4

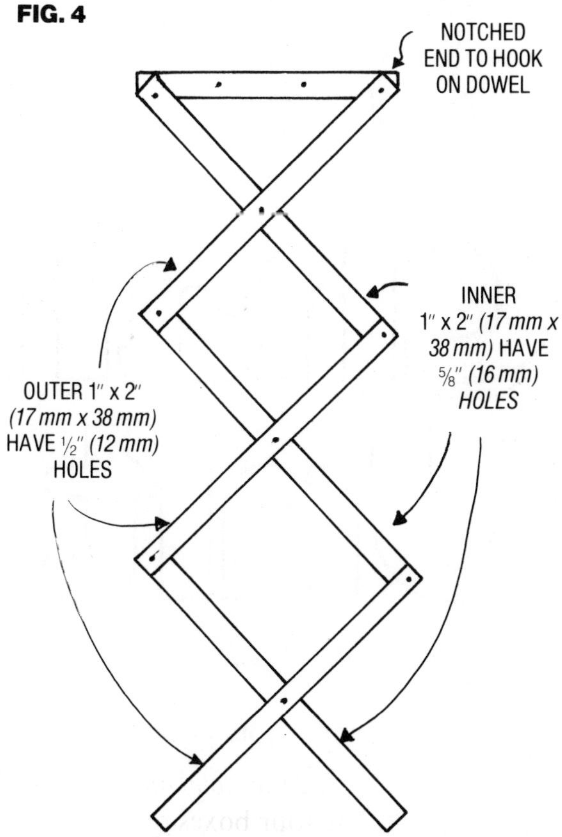

FIG. 5

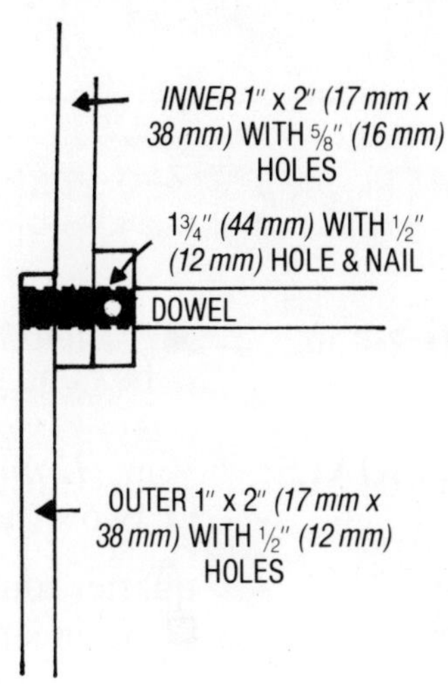

3

Changing Unit

This unit is made up of four boxes stacked two high to provide a counter 24 in. *(600 mm)* wide and 36 in. *(900 mm)* long. The four boxes offer plenty of deep storage space for diapers and other necessities, and the surface area is long enough to accommodate a two-year-old.

The advantage of using these boxes over the standard changing table is that when the baby has outgrown the need for changing, the boxes are practical for toy storage, seating or any other application you can think of.

I used particle board because it is priced at less than half the cost of plywood. It is strong and durable and looks good when painted.

When the boxes are stacked, the top will be 34 in. *(850 mm)* from the floor. If you are short you might find this too high. In that case, cut down all the pieces that are 16 in. *(400 mm)* wide, including the back pieces, to 15 in. *(375 mm)*, giving a height of 32 in. *(800 mm)*.

What You Need

TOOLS: saw, square, drill and No. 6 combination countersink drill bit, hammer, miter box and saw, screwdriver

MATERIALS:

½ in. *(12 mm)* particle board
- ☐ two sheets 4 ft. x 8 ft. *(1200 mm x 2400 mm)*

quarter round
- ☐ 32 linear ft. *(9.6 m)*

flat-head wood screws
- ☐ one hundred 1 in. *(25 mm)* No. 6
- ☐ four ¾ in. *(20 mm)* No. 6
- ☐ 1½ in. *(40 mm)* finishing nails
- ☐ wood filler

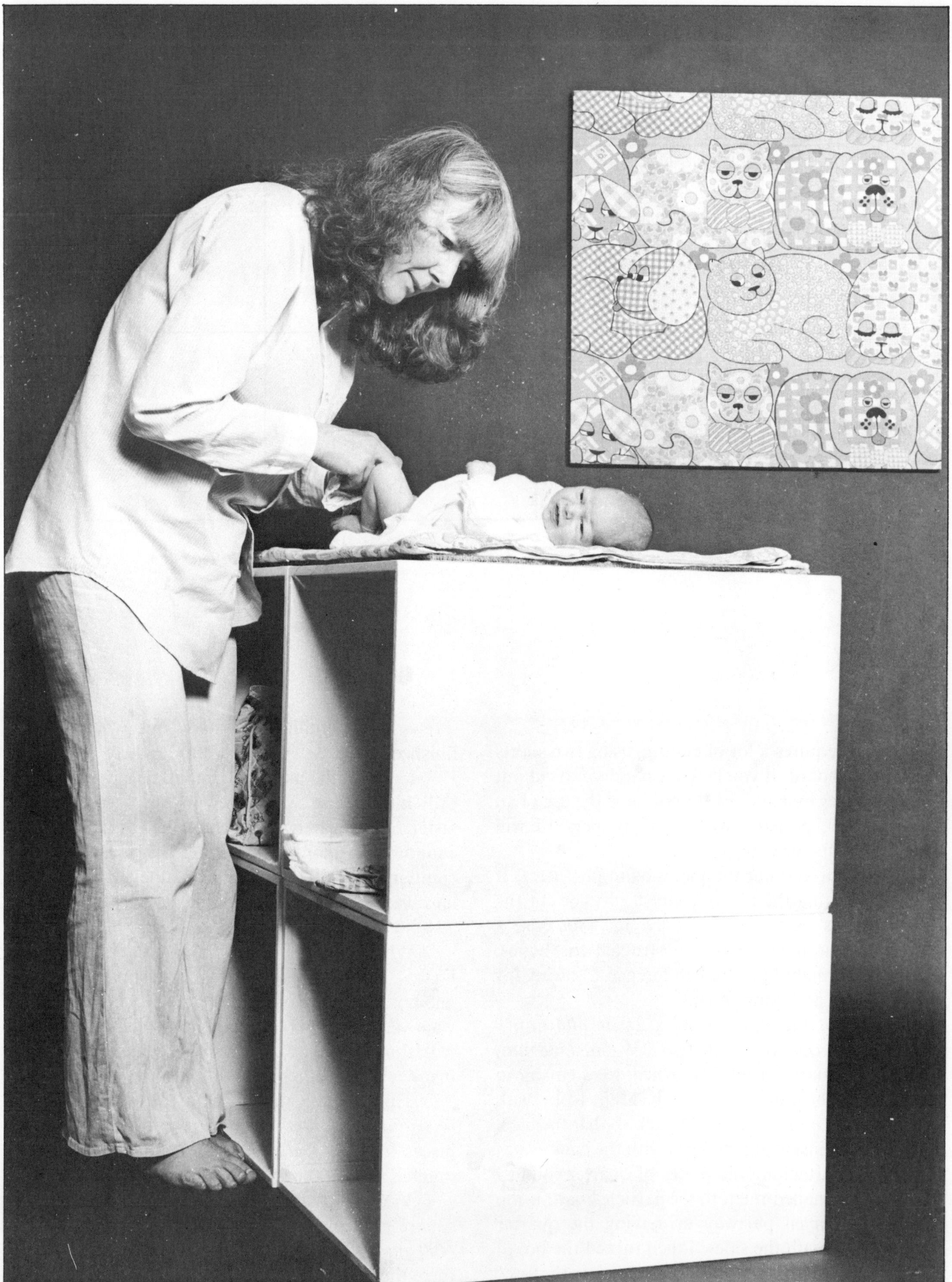

FIG. 1A

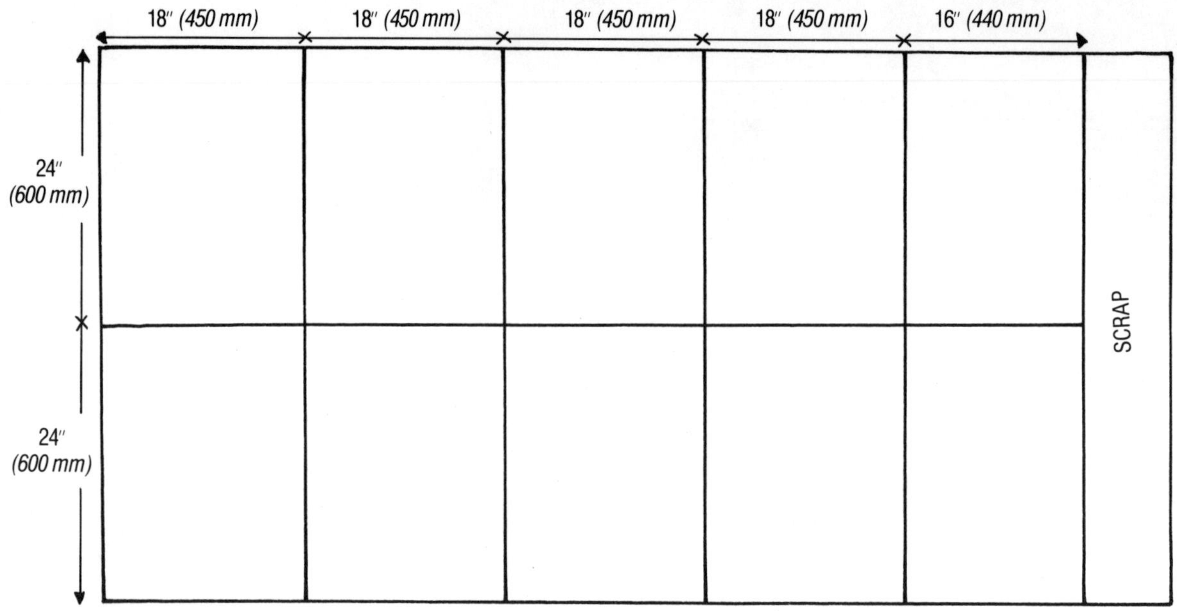

Building Instructions

This item requires a lot of cutting, using two sheets of particle board. If you lack the patience to cut out all the pieces by hand, or do not have the use of an electric saw, perhaps your local lumberyard will make the cuts for you.

Lay out and cut the pieces as in FIGURE 1. If you are cutting the pieces yourself, do not cut the back pieces—the 16 in. x 17 in. *(400 mm x 576 mm)*—until you have constructed the boxes, since there might be a small difference, allowing for the saw kerf and minor errors.

Each of the eight 16 in. x 24 in. *(400 mm x 600 mm)* pieces will have two 23½ in. *(588 mm)* pieces of quarter round attached to them as in FIGURE 2. The mitered end will be at the front, with the ½ in. *(12 mm)* space at the back so that the back piece can fit inside and be flush with the back.

When attaching the pieces of quarter round I temporarily nailed them to the particle board using two nails driven partway in, having the quarter round flush with the sides. I then turned the board over and drilled and fastened them with three screws each, pulling the nails out when I had finished.

I specify the use of a combination countersink drill bit because working with this tool is much faster and neater than changing drill bits for countersink, shank and pilot holes. Combination countersink drill bits are available at any good hardware store for a reasonable price. Be sure to get a No. 6 bit for the No. 6 screws.

When the quarter round is attached to two boards 16 in. *(400 mm)* wide, begin construction of one box by laying one of the pieces 18 in. *(450 mm)* wide vertically next to the quarter round and fasten with three screws. Attach a similar piece in the same manner on the other side.

Tip the whole thing over and lay another 16 in. *(400 mm)* piece between the two 18 in. *(450 mm)* pieces to form the other side. Be sure you get the mitered ends at the front. Attach with the screws.

Your four-sided box might not be perfectly square, but if the back piece—16 in. x 17 in. *(400 mm x 576 mm)*—is cut at right angles, it will force the box square.

FIG. 1B

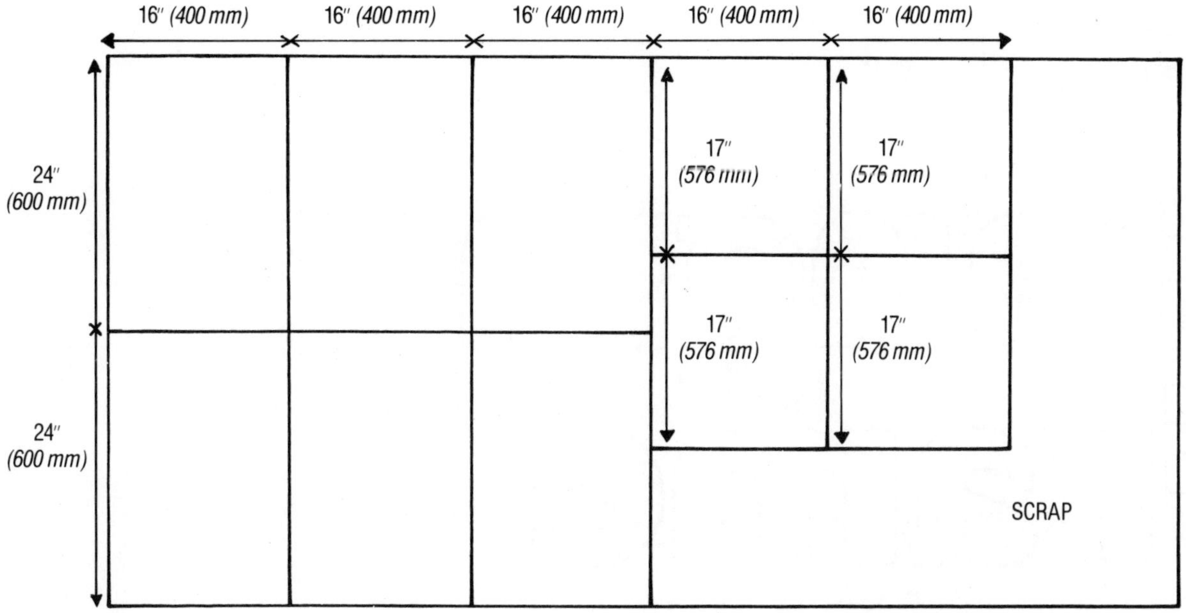

3—Fig 1 (B)

FIG. 2

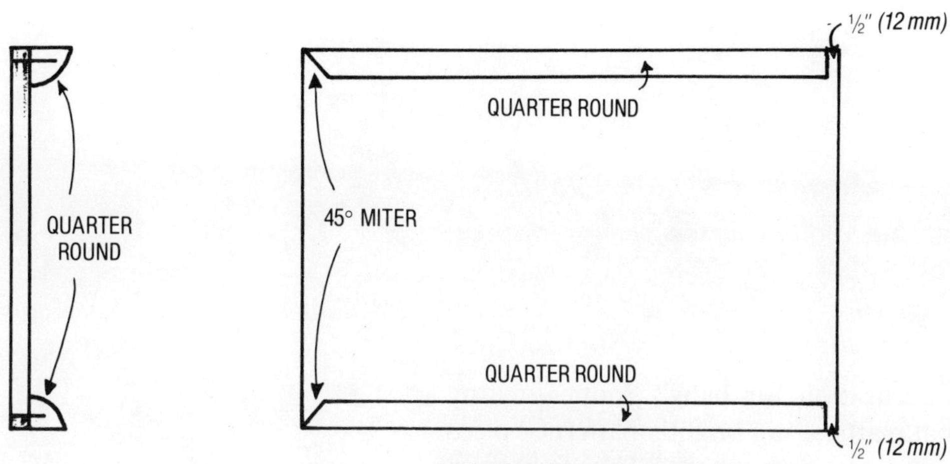

QUARTER ROUND FLUSH WITH SIDES, BUT ½″ (12 mm) SHORT AT BACK END.

The back piece must fit very snugly, so you may have to measure it to be sure of a tight fit. When it is in place it should slide inside the four sides, flush with the back, and be held from going any farther in by the quarter round. Set two nails in from the sides into the edge of the back piece.

After filling all the screw holes and gaps, I sanded and gave the boxes a coat of undercoat paint, then a coat of semigloss enamel, inside and out.

When you stack the boxes for use, you should attach them to each other with a screw going from each box into the one beside and above or below it. Attaching them in this manner ensures that the boxes will not slide apart.

A scrap of carpet tacked to the top makes a nice pad. Cover with waterproof cloth—leatherette or a plastic groundsheet—and the unit is ready for baby's first changing.

4

Hanging Frame

A cheerful decoration for baby's room—or any other, for that matter—is a brightly patterned piece of cloth stretched on a frame. This light and inexpensive decoration is easily made at home.

What You Need

TOOLS: heavy-duty stapler or staple gun, Surform file, square, drill and ¼ in. *(6 mm)* bit, miter box and saw, two clamps

MATERIALS:

- ☐ 1 in. x 2 in. *(17 mm x 38 mm)* pine or fir of good quality (clear)
- ☐ ¼ in. *(6 mm)* dowel
- ☐ brightly patterned cloth

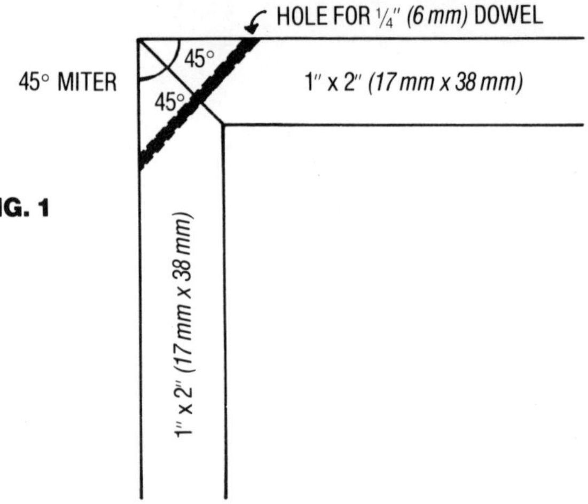

FIG. 1

FIG. 2

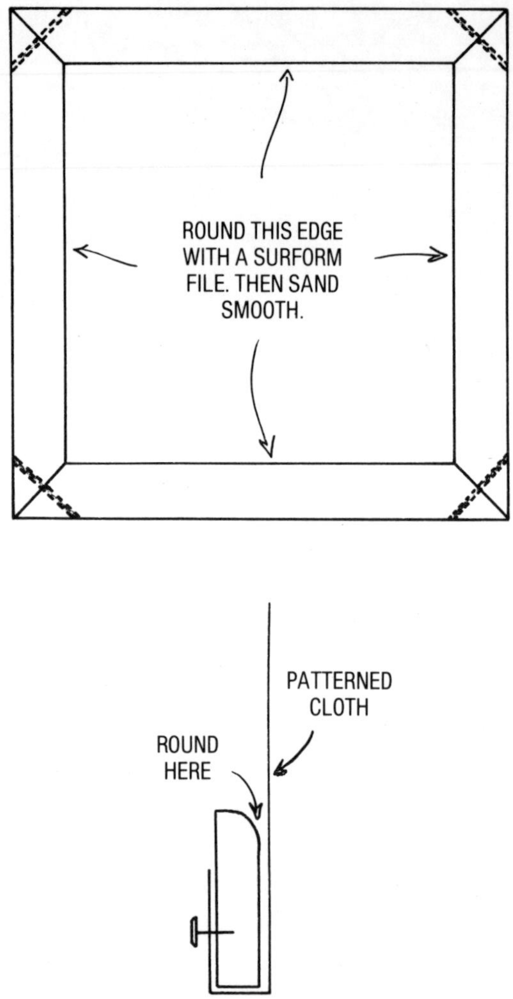

Building Instructions

Buy the cloth first, keeping in mind that you will need at least 1½ in. *(40 mm)* on each edge to pull over the frame. Buy enough 1 in. x 2 in. *(17 mm x 38 mm)* softwood to go around the perimeter of the pattern of cloth you wish to have showing.

Cut the 1 in. x 2 in. *(17 mm x 38 mm)* on a 45° angle using your miter box. When cutting the wood, remember that you can turn over the adjoining piece from one cut to make a 90° angle.

The easiest way to hold the pieces while drilling the holes through the corners is to clamp the 1 in. x 2 in. *(17 mm x 38 mm)* to a square-cornered piece of plywood. Then drill the hole through the corner as in **FIGURE 1**. The hole should be roughly in the center of the edges of the 1 in. x 2 in. *(17 mm x 38 mm)* and 90° to the miter joint. Do not worry too much about being exact: if the miter is cut accurately, the pieces clamped properly and the dowel inserted as soon as the hole is drilled, there should be no mistakes. Cut the dowel to length as each hole is drilled, since length may vary.

Each joint in itself will turn, but when all four corners are made in the above manner the frame will be held rigid.

After all four corners have been drilled and doweled, take the Surform file and round the inner corner on the flat of the 1 in. x 2 in. *(17 mm x 38 mm)* against which the cloth will lay, and sand smooth. This is to prevent that edge from showing once the cloth is stretched. (See **FIGURE 2**.)

Begin stretching the cloth by laying it face-down on the tabletop. Center the frame on the back side of the cloth with the rounded edge lying against it. Staple the cloth at the midpoint on each side with a few staples, pulling it taut but not too much.

Work around the sides, from the center to the corners, stretching the cloth in stages with a staple about every 1 in. or 2 in. *(25 mm or 50 mm)*. Do not try to staple all of one side and then all of another side: the pattern will become distorted and you will have to start over again.

When you get to the corners, fold and tuck them neatly, securing them with several staples.

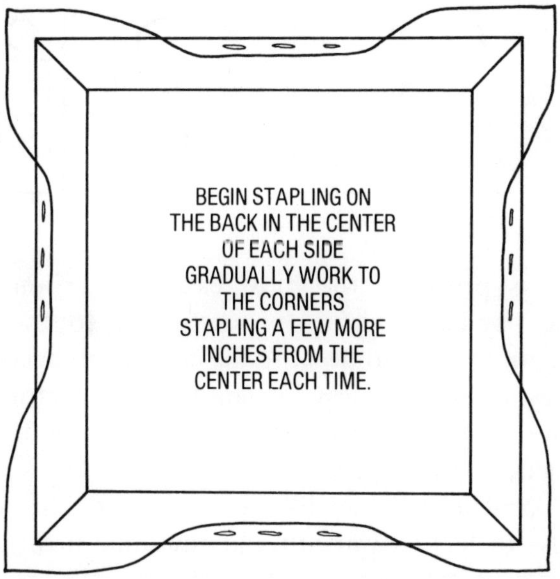

FIG. 3

5 Sling

This is probably the most easily made and inexpensive baby carrier. It is useful only for the first four months or so because the child soon becomes heavy and too restless to want to stay in it for any period of time. But for those first few months the sling can be a godsend.

Newborn babies like to be close to the adult body, to feel its warmth and rhythmic breathing. We found that when Penny—and later, Peter—was carried around in the sling, she was much happier and also slept more than if left in her cradle. We could carry her around the house, or when doing errands, and still have both hands free while she was in a contented slumber.

Because the one piece of cloth makes two slings, one can be adjusted for each parent.

What You Need

TOOLS: scissors

MATERIALS:
- ☐ one piece of cloth 42 in. *(1065 mm)* wide and 2 yd. *(2 m)* long
- ☐ two large safety pins

Building Instructions

Cut the cloth as in **FIGURE 1**.

Knot corners *A* and *B* together for each sling using a square knot. Put the sling over your head and shoulder as if you were going to cradle your right arm in it, with corner *C* near your right elbow.

Put the baby in the sling with his head at your left side, then pin up corner *C* so that he is held firmly in the sling. If you do not pin up corner *C*, the baby could slide out. We pinned up the corner of Penny's sling so that her bottom was nicely cradled in the curve of the cloth.

You must undo the pin when taking the baby out, but the spot where the pin goes in soon becomes well marked. Once used to sliding the baby into and out of the sling, you will find it a very handy item.

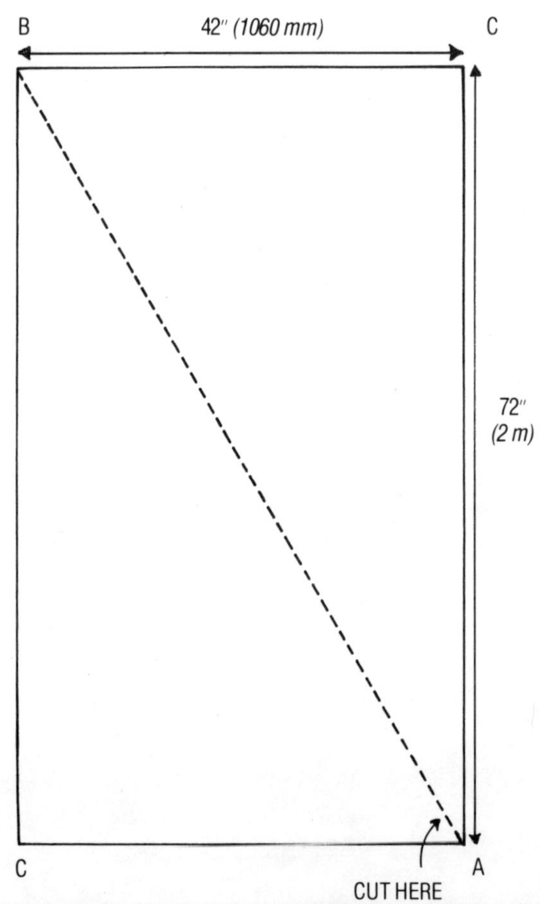

6 Faces

TRIANGLE CIRCLE

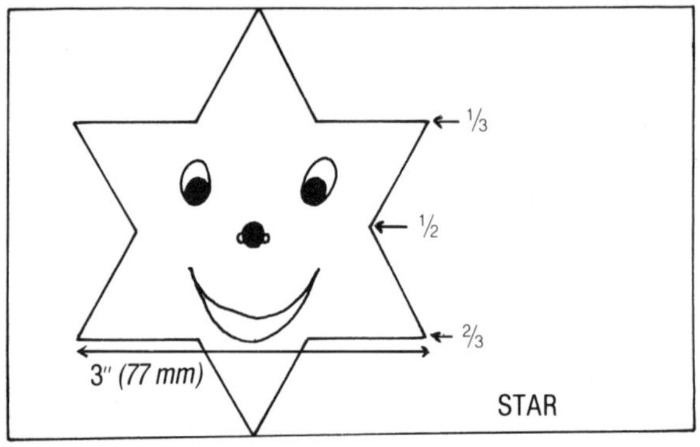

STAR

OVAL

Building Instructions

To make interesting things for Penny to look at, I simply took a few pieces of scrap pine and cut them into geometric shapes: one oval, one circle, one triangle and one six-pointed star (two equilateral triangles superimposed on each other). These are easy shapes to make. I used 1 in. x 4 in. *(17 mm x 89 mm)* scraps, so the four pieces were a maximum width of that size wood.

We were surprised at how soon Penny began to play with the shapes. In her second week she started reaching out and batting at them with her little fist. We found that since small babies lie on their sides, she was attracted to the shapes more when they were tied to the side dowels of her crib than when they were hanging overhead.

I painted faces on the shapes to strengthen the early bonding process whereby the baby recognizes faces before other objects. Using bright red and yellow paint I gave two of the shapes yellow eyes and mouth on a red background, while the others had the reverse color scheme. Penny seemed to be attracted to the yellow face with the red features more than the others, although this was also the largest face.

In her book *Teach Your Baby*, Dr. Genevieve Painter recommends that bright objects be kept 12 in. *(305 mm)* from the bridge of the baby's nose, enabling him to focus on them easily. We found that Penny was attracted to things at that distance, but we also put the toys within her reach, about 9 in. *(230 mm)* away, so that she could amuse herself by touching them.

The shapes were hung from a center point with the faces looking at her. Most crib mobiles seem to be made for the adults to admire; they generally face someone looking at them on their own level, not the baby who looks up from below.

I drilled a ¼ in. *(6 mm)* hole in the center of each shape and then used a short piece of braided nylon rope, ⅛ in. or 3/16 in. *(3 mm or 4 mm)* in diameter, with an overhand knot in it for a stopper. On some of the pieces I let a rope hang out from the knot 2 in. to 3 in. *(50 mm to 75 mm)* for the baby to grab at.

Even at the early age of two weeks Penny seemed to appreciate her crib toys.

7 Napping Cot

Since when she was very young Penny spent part of the day with her mother at the office, I built this napping cot with the sit-up addition to fit on Fiona's desk. Penny was content with the arrangement until she reached the restless age of six months, when nothing could keep her confined.

The cot can be built to any dimension and with some modifications can be useful for children up to six years of age. It could be used at a nursery school, for young children at grandmother's house or at the baby sitter's. It also makes a good doll bed, since it is strong enough for the child to climb in with the dolls.

Because the cot has low sides, infants of four to nine months need supervision to prevent them from toppling out until they get big enough to climb in and out at will.

The cot is economical to build. Its sling-type mattress support is much more comfortable than a slab of plywood; many sailors have slept on a pipe berth or root berth constructed in much the same manner.

What You Need

TOOLS: saw, miter box, drill and ¾ in. *(18 mm)* bit

MATERIALS: 2 in. x 2 in. *(38 mm x 38 mm)* softwood (pine or fir)

- ☐ two pieces 14 in. *(355 mm)*
- ☐ two pieces 12 in. *(305 mm)*

¾ in. *(18 mm)* softwood dowels

- ☐ seven 18 in. *(457 mm)*
- ☐ six 29 in. *(737 mm)*

- ☐ Glue
- ☐ Fabric-backed plastic cloth, 30 in. x 32 in. *(762 mm x 812 mm)*
- ☐ ten ⅜ in. *(9 mm)* grommets (reinforcing eyelets)
- ☐ ¼ in. *(6 mm)* rope (nylon or plastic), approx. 10 ft. *(3 m)* long
- ☐ 1 in. *(25 mm)* foam pad, 20 in. x 30 in. *(510 mm x 762 mm)*

Optional: set of four plastic mirror holders

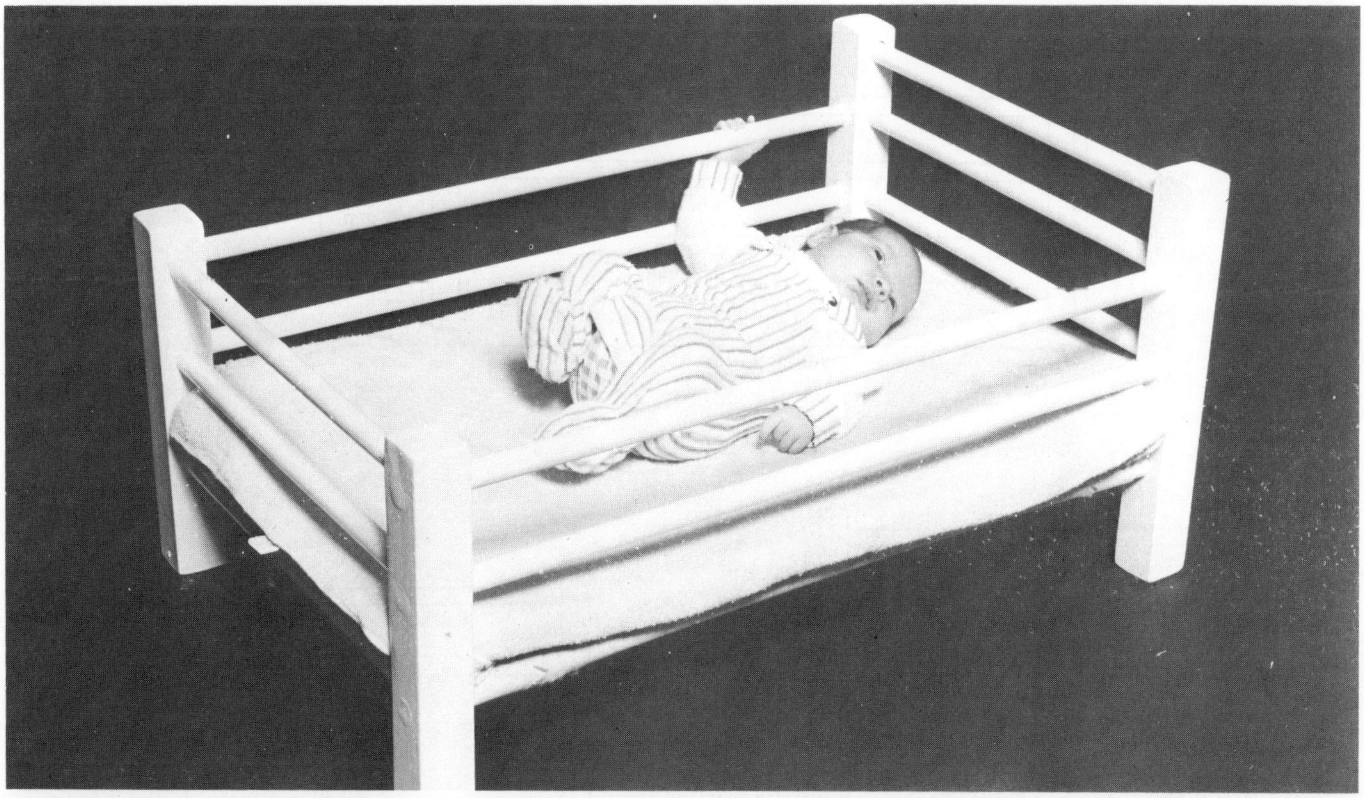

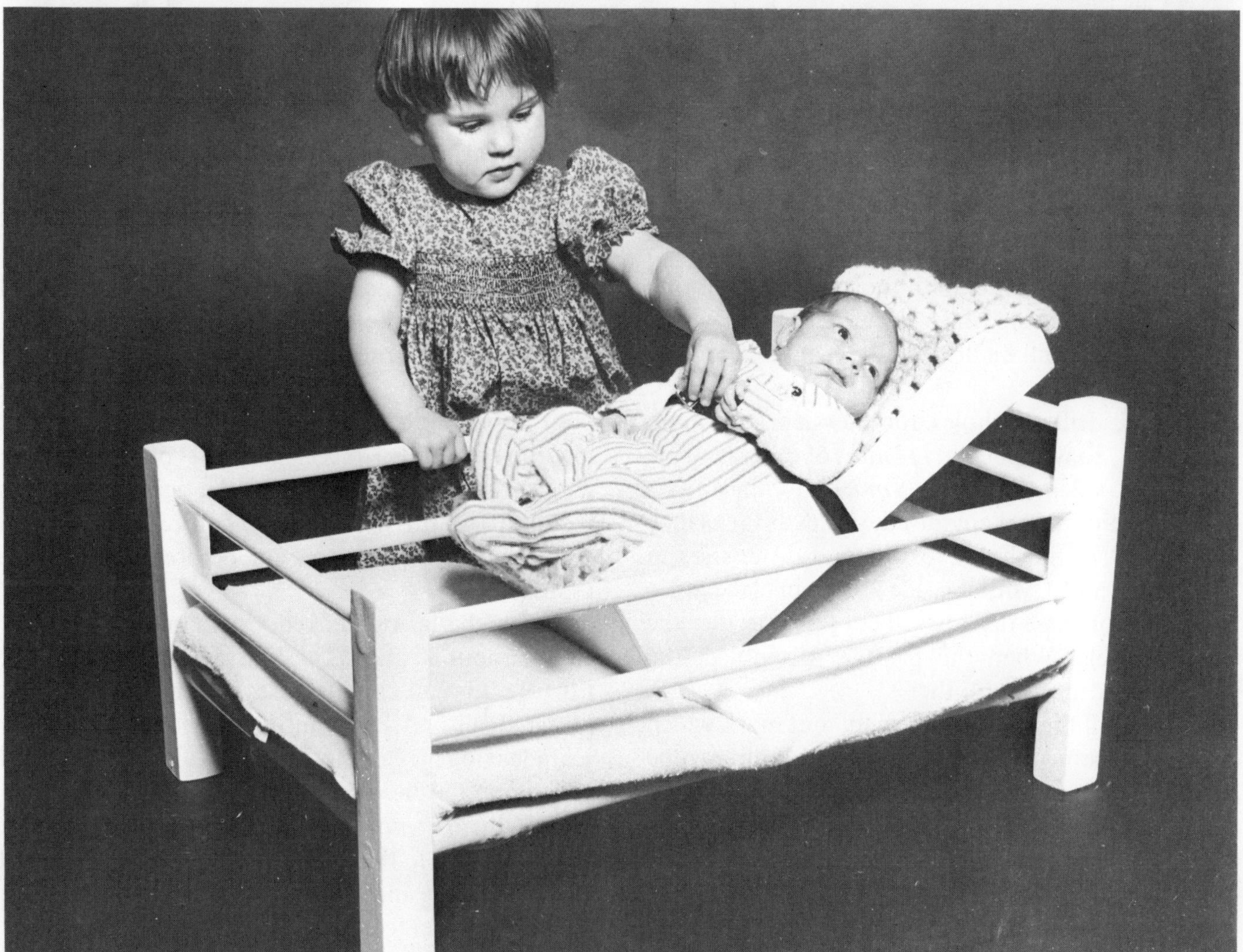

FIG. 1

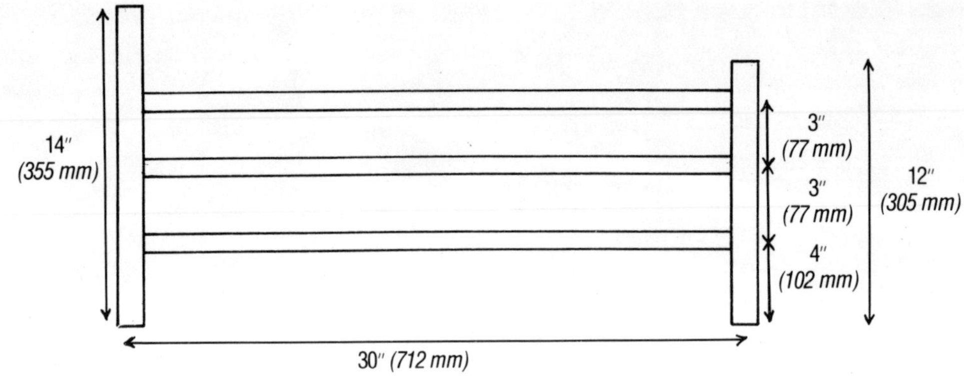

FIG. 2

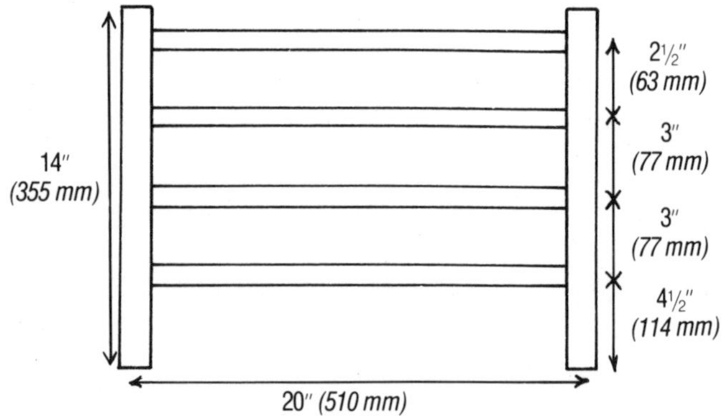

FIG. 3

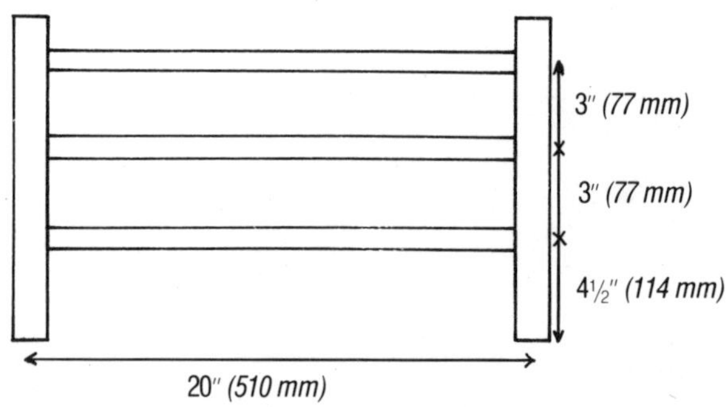

Building Instructions

Cut the 2 in. x 2 in. *(38 mm x 38 mm)* pieces to length. Mark the center of the holes on them, noting that you must decide which corner each piece will be in, since holes will be drilled into two sides of each piece.

First, drill the holes for the side bars as in **FIGURE 1**, to within 1/2 in. *(12 mm)* of the other side of the 2 in. x 2 in. *(38 mm x 38 mm)*. Give the dowels a trial fit, jamming them into the holes as far as they will go. Drill the holes for the end dowels, as in **FIGURES 2** and **3**, with the side dowels in place, since the holes for these dowels will cut partway into the other dowels. When the piece is assembled, the dowels lock into each other.

Take all the dowels out again, but mark which holes they came from. Each dowel will have to be returned to its original hole.

Put a few drops of glue on the end of each dowel and into each hole as you begin to reassemble the pieces. Be sure that the notched parts of the side dowels are in the proper position when assembling, so that the end dowels can slot into them.

When everything is assembled, put the cot on a flat-topped table, place a board across it and set a cement block on the board. This ensures that the glue will dry with the legs flat on the tabletop, and that the finished cot will not wobble.

The cot should, of course, be rectangular, and it will be if your holes were properly drilled. But if you find that the corners are not square you must pull it into shape, which can be easily done using your rope. Tie the rope around the 2 in. x 2 in. *(38 mm x 38 mm)* pieces that are on the longest diagonal. Make a loop and wind it tight until the cot is square. All this must be done before the glue dries.

Sand and paint the cot before installing the mattress support.

Cut the fabric-backed vinyl cloth or Leatherette to about 30 in. x 32 in. *(762 mm x 812 mm)*. (See **FIGURE 4**.) You can also use a heavy cotton if you prefer. Roll under the unfinished edge, then sew a seam leaving a 1 1/2 in. to 2 in. *(38 mm to 50 mm)* hem all around the cloth so that it is finished at about 24 in. x 26 in. *(610 mm x 660 mm)*. Put grommets in the hem as shown in the diagram.

Install the mattress support by sliding it over the lower dowel from the side, pulling the grommets along the edge to the underside. Tie one end of the

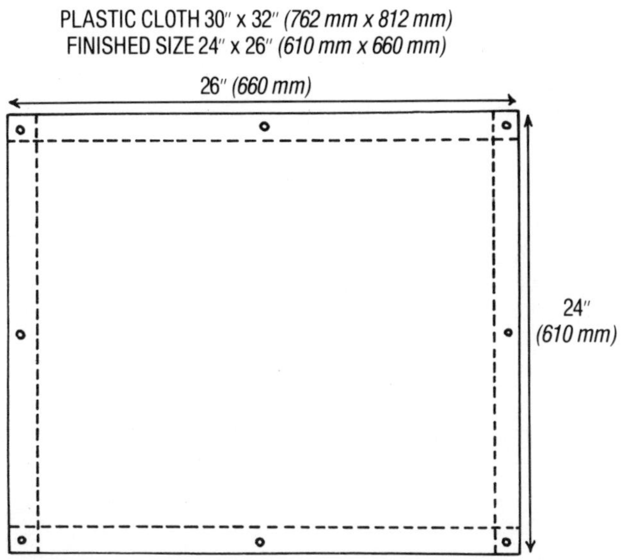

FIG. 4

rope to one of the corner grommets, then thread it to the other grommets along the sides. Pull them fairly tight and knot the end. The two grommets along the end should have a short piece of rope tying them to the end dowels.

I cut the foam to the total outside dimensions of the cot—20 in. x 30 in. *(510 mm x 762 mm)*—and then cut the corners out to fit around the 2 in. x 2 in. *(38 mm x 38 mm)*. A waterproof covering should be put over the foam mattress.

When the cot was placed on Fiona's desk, we found that if the baby jumped around in it a lot, or if someone bumped it, the legs at one end would slide off the edge and Penny would get a jolt from falling the 4 in. *(100 mm)* to the dowel. I installed a set of four plastic mirror holders on the ends of the legs on the outside. These holders over the edge of the desk prevented the cot from sliding off.

The holders were installed with one screw each. When the cot was moved to a flat surface, the screws could be loosened and the holders turned sideways so that the cot would sit flat on the legs.

SIT-UP ADDITION

The sit-up is patterned after those molded plastic seats that are so popular. I made this addition to the cot because when Penny was two and a half months old she became bored with lying down all the time. Thus a two-function unit takes up the space of one unit.

What You Need

TOOLS: saw, miter box, drill and ¾ in. *(18 mm)* bit

MATERIALS:

½ in. *(12 mm)* plywood
- ☐ one piece 19½ in. x 9 in. *(495 mm x 228 mm)*
- ☐ one piece 5¾ in. x 9 in. *(147 mm x 228 mm)*
- ☐ one piece approx. 8 in. x 30 in. *(204 mm x 762 mm),* to be cut later

¾ in. x ¾ in. *(17 mm x 17 mm)* pine
- ☐ one piece 18½ in. *(470 mm)*
- ☐ two pieces 18¼ in. *(464 mm)*

2 in. x 2 in. *(38 mm x 38 mm)* pine or fir
- ☐ one piece 7½ in. *(190 mm)*

- ☐ 1¼ in. *(32 mm)* finishing nails
- ☐ glue
- ☐ safety belt (To hold the baby in the seat, we used a strap and buckle from an old backpack, but a belt or strip of cloth will do.)

FIG. 1

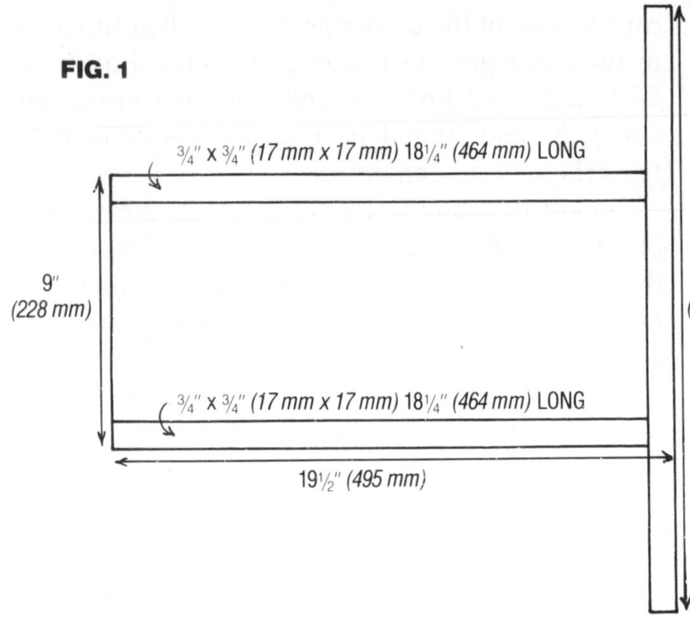

FIG. 2

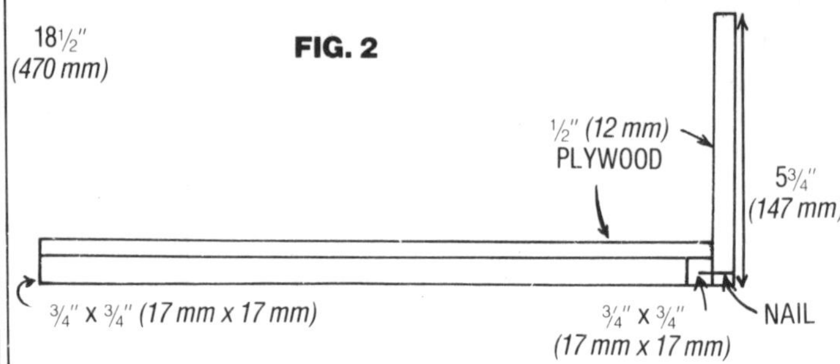

FIG. 3

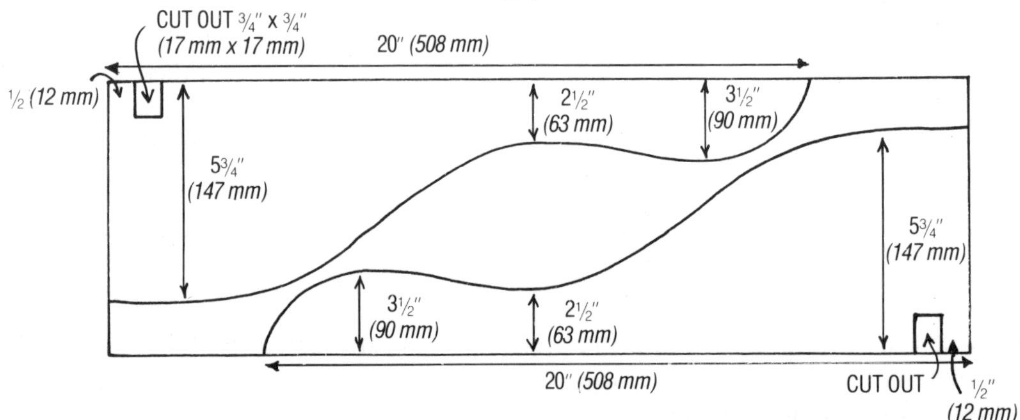

Building Instructions

Begin by cutting the 19½ in. x 9 in. *(495 mm x 228 mm)* and 5¾ in. x 9 in. *(147 mm x 228 mm)* plywood and the three pieces of ¾ in. x ¾ in. *(17 mm x 17 mm)* pine. Nail and glue the ¾ in. x ¾ in. *(17 mm x 17 mm)* pieces to the bottom side of the 19½ in. *(495 mm)* plywood piece as in **FIGURE 1**. Use one nail every 3 in. *(77 mm)*.

Attach the 5¾ in. x 9 in. *(147 mm x 228 mm)* piece as in **FIGURE 2**, using glue and nails in the same manner.

Lay out the 8 in. x 30 in. *(204 mm x 762 mm)* piece as in **FIGURE 3**. You will need either a coping saw or a jigsaw to cut these two pieces apart. If you are using a coping saw, you will have to swivel the blade around as you cut. When you get to the wide part, start from the other end and cut in until you meet the place you left off.

The notch is to accommodate the ¾ in. x ¾ in. *(17 mm x 17 mm)* piece at the seat end. This should be a close fit. Make the cuts in from the end with your coping saw, then make the inner cut by swiveling the blade around the corner and making short cuts.

Glue and nail the sides to the ¾ in. x ¾ in. *(17 mm x 17 mm)* pieces and to the end plywood piece that makes the seat.

Glue and nail the 2 in. x 2 in. *(38 mm x 38 mm)* piece at the upper end between the ¾ in. x ¾ in. *(17 mm x 17 mm)* pieces, but flush with the end of the plywood. The 2 in. x 2 in. *(38 mm x 38 mm)* hooks over the top rail of the cot at the head end after the ¾ in. x ¾ in. *(17 mm x 17 mm)* piece is set on the mattress and turned to sit on the lower dowel.

The safety strap to hold the baby in should fit around under the arms and across the chest. Simply tack it in place on the outside of the chair. We used a quilt draped over the whole chair for cushioning. A piece of foam with a plastic cover could also be used.

Penny's sit-up was painted white.

8 'Jail Bars' Standard Crib

This piece conforms to the specifications set down in the Canadian Hazardous Products Act for safety in infant cribs. The bars are sufficiently close together that the baby's head cannot slip between them. The sides are high enough to be safe for a child up to 35 in. *(890 mm)* tall, the height of an average two-year-old. The gate does not slide all the way to the surface of the mattress, but conforms to the standard of being 9 in. *(230 mm)* high when completely lowered.

When Penny started to sleep in her crib at the ripe old age of two months, she looked very small for such a large cage. But we did have the comfort of knowing that for some time to come she would be safe when we put her to bed.

This is a moderately complicated piece to build and should not be undertaken by the beginning carpenter. I will not go into a detailed description of its construction because anyone building it should have some experience in putting things together. Building and finishing the crib took nearly thirty hours.

What You Need

TOOLS: saw, square, chisel, drill and bits, miter box, backsaw or miter saw, hammer, plane

MATERIALS: 2 in. x 2 in. *(38 mm x 38 mm)* softwood (fir or pine)

- ☐ eleven pieces 47 in. *(1195 mm)*
- ☐ six pieces 27 in. *(685 mm)*
- ☐ one piece 43½ in. *(1110 mm)*

¾ in. *(18 mm)* softwood dowels

- ☐ twenty-five 28 in. *(710 mm)* for the ends and gate
- ☐ fourteen 24¾ in. *(630 mm)* for the back
- ☐ two 45¼ in. *(1150 mm)* for the slides
- ☐ two 20 in. *(508 mm)*
- ☐ one 42 in. *(1067 mm)* for the mattress support
- ☐ scrap for ten 1¾ in. *(38 mm)* pieces

¼ in. *(6 mm)* hex-head bolts and nuts

- ☐ ten 3½ in. *(90 mm)*
- ☐ four 4 in. *(100 mm)*
- ☐ twenty-four flat washers for above
- ☐ two 1 in. *(25 mm)* No. 8 flat-head wood screws
- ☐ four casters, pin type, 2 in. *(50 mm)* wheels
- ☐ 10 oz. canvas or fabric-backed Leatherette, 48 in. x 32 in. *(1200 mm x 860 mm)*
- ☐ 3 in. *(75 mm)* foam, 20 in. x 40 in. *(510 mm x 1010 mm)*
- ☐ ¼ in. *(6 mm)* nylon or other synthetic cord, 8 ft. *(2400 mm)* long
- ☐ four ¼ in. x 2 in. *(6 mm x 50 mm)* eyebolts with eight flat washers

FIG. 1

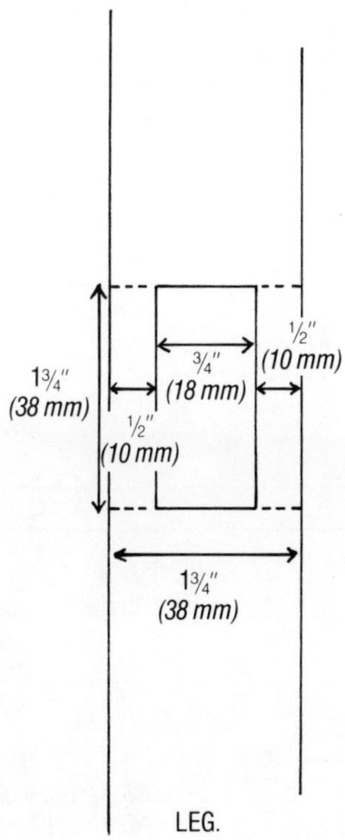

FIG. 2

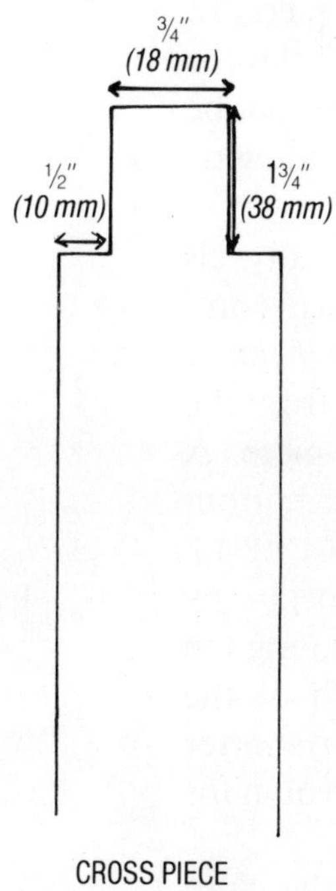

FIG. 3

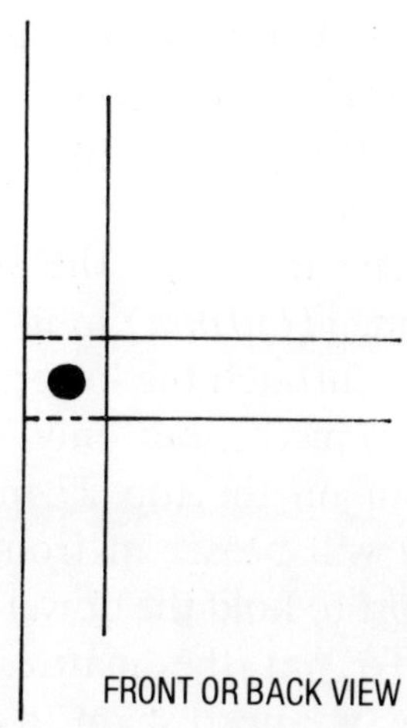

Building Instructions

Begin by cutting nine of the 47 in. *(1195 mm)* pieces. These are the four legs and five crosspieces. The five crosspieces will be set into the legs with open mortise and tenon joints. See **FIGURE 1** and the "Wood Joints" section, which discusses mortise and tenon joints.

When the mortise and tenon joints fit together nicely, remove the upper 2 in. x 2 in. *(38 mm x 38 mm)* on the back piece and drill the holes for the dowels. These should be on 3 in. *(77 mm)* centers beginning 3 in. *(77 mm)* from the shoulders of the tenon and ¾ in. *(20 mm)* deep along the centerline of the 2 in. x 2 in. *(38 mm x 38 mm)*. Wrap a piece of masking tape around your drill so that you will know when the holes are ¾ in. *(20 mm)* deep.

Assemble the back piece, gluing both the

dowels and the mortise and tenon joints and setting the dowels in the joints. Be sure that the piece is square and flat.

Cut the 27 in. *(685 mm)* pieces of 2 in. x 2 in. *(38 mm x 38 mm)* and cut the half-lap joint in these and the underside of the lower crossbars on the front and back pieces as in **FIGURE 2**. When these are cut and matched up, drill the holes for the dowels on 3 in. *(77 mm)* centers. Set the dowels with glue and bolt the ends to the side pieces as in **FIGURE 2** countersinking the bolts at both the head and nut end.

Bolt the bottom brace across the ends, flush with the bottom of the legs, countersinking the bolts. Then bolt the $43\frac{1}{2}$ in. *(1110 mm)* spreader in place between these bottom two braces at the center.

The remaining two 47 in. *(1195 mm)* 2 in. x 2 in. *(38 mm x 38 mm)* are for the horizontal pieces of the gate. Cut these to length and drill the holes for the dowels as in **FIGURE 3**. Glue the dowels, but be sure that the gate is square and flat before the glue sets.

The holes for the vertical slide—the dowels $45\frac{1}{4}$ in. *(1150 mm)* long—should be drilled completely through the lower two 2 in. x 2 in. *(38 mm x 38 mm)* pieces, but only $\frac{3}{4}$ in. *(20 mm)* in from the bottom on the top 27 in. *(685 mm)* end piece. A screw will be set in from the side of the bottom support to hold the dowel in place. (See **FIGURE 4**.)

To put the mattress support in, begin by sewing a lapped seam to receive a dowel along the two ends and the back side. The length of the finished cloth should be about 1 in. *(25 mm)* shorter than the inside length of the crib, to allow room for adjustment as the fabric stretches.

Make three evenly spaced holes in the cloth along each end. These can be burned in the Leatherette or simply pierced in the cotton. The hole edges should be saturated with glue to prevent fraying, and the holes made so that all of the tension on the cord to pass through them will be on the dowels and not on the cloth. Lace the cord around the dowel in the cloth and around the upright dowels in the ends.

Push the cloth between the two horizontal braces in the back and insert the 40 in. *(1010 mm)* dowel into the seam. Then, with the crib upside down, pull the cloth tight over the bottom horizontal brace at the front and, beginning in the center,

FIG. 2

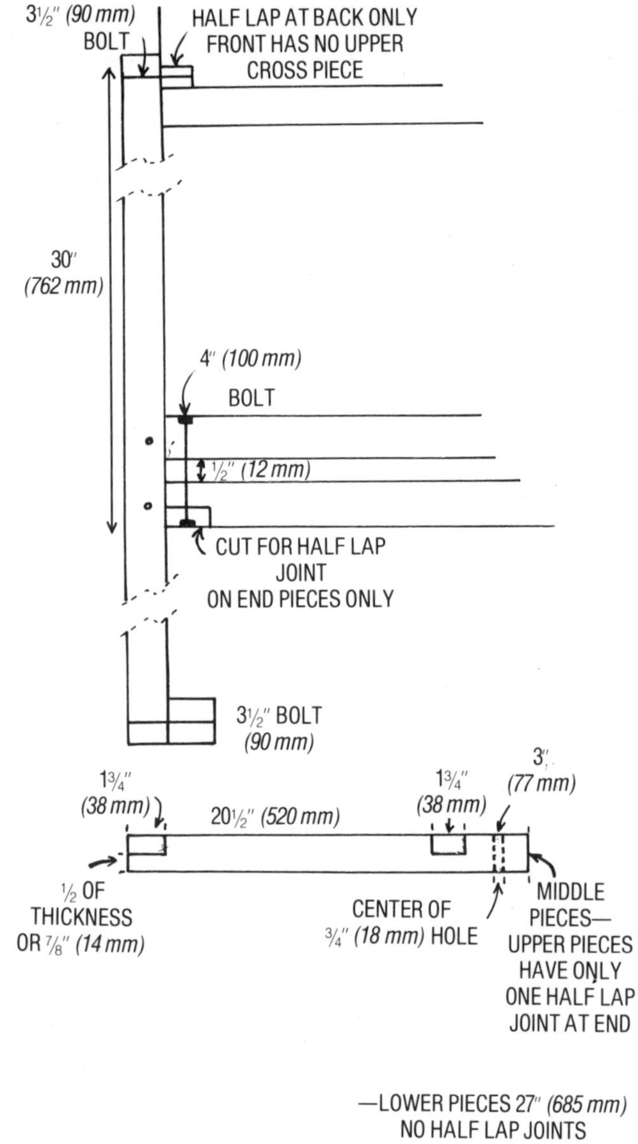

tack the fabric to the underside (now the top side) of the 2 in. x 2 in. *(38 mm x 38 mm)*. If the cloth stretches after the baby has slept in the crib for some time, simply take out the tacks and pull tight again.

You could also cut a piece of plywood to fit the bottom for a mattress support. In this case a thicker mattress pad is required.

Cut a piece of 3 in. *(77 mm)* foam to fit tightly around the inside of the crib, and cover it with a waterproof sheet.

Before painting, cut all bolt ends flush with the wood surface with a hacksaw, and file smooth. The

FIG. 3

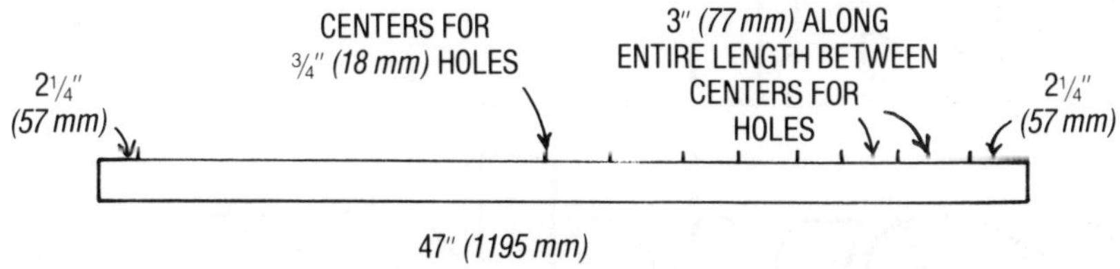

FIG. 4

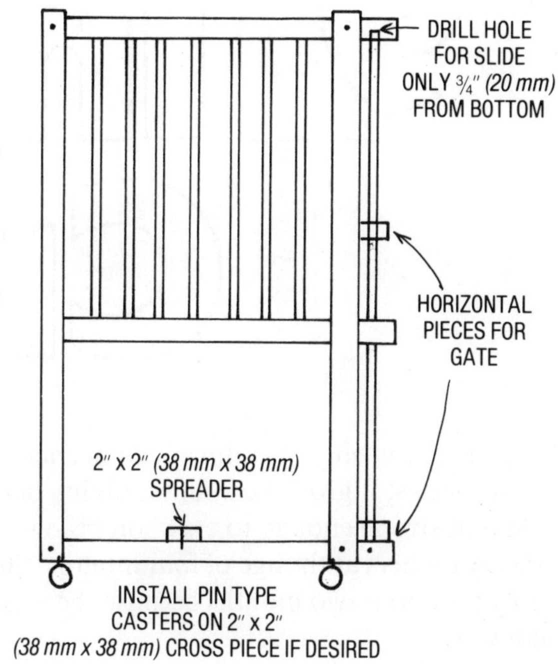

nut and head should be below the surface in countersunk holes. These holes can be filled with wood filler, or left as is and painted over.

For latches to hold the sliding gate closed (up), I used four ¼ in. *(6 mm)* eyebolts with 2 in. *(50 mm)* shank with two flat washers and one nut each.

Drill a hole through the top crosspiece at its center, roughly over the center of the top rail on the gate. Slide a flat washer over the bolt, to the eye end, then insert the bolt into the hole with the eye end toward the outside. Put another flat washer on the bolt, then tighten with the flat of the eye vertical.

Raise the gate and hold another eyebolt beside the one bolted on. The flats of the eyes should line up close together when the other eyebolt is in place in the top rail of the gate. It does not matter on which side of the first the second eyebolt is, but do not have them too close to the upright behind them.

Mark the hole by tapping the eyebolt with a hammer, then drill and install as above. Do the same on the other side.

To hold the gate up, I clipped the eyebolts together on each side with a dog-chain snap. You must find a fairly large one to snap over the two eyebolts. Because there are several different types and sizes of chains, try the snaps at the store when buying the eyebolts.

To keep the dog-chain snap near the eyebolts when it's not done up, you tie it with a piece of light cord to the cross-piece behind the upright.

Saw off the bolt ends flush with the nut, then file smooth. The nuts may need periodic tightening, since an active child will rattle the gate a lot.

9 Infant Crawler

This article is often recommended in child-development books; it gives the infant mobility before he is old and strong enough to crawl on his own. We put Penny on hers at the age of four months. She used it only for about two months because she was an early crawler.

The infant lies on his stomach on the crawler with his head over the wider end and the narrower end between his legs. He is supported off the floor and can scoot along by pushing with his hands and legs without having to lift his body. The head end is long enough that if the child runs into a wall, the crawler will hit it before his head touches it.

A carpeted floor is a disadvantage since the infant does not have the strength to push the casters through the pile of the carpet, and ends up going in circles. Bare floors are better.

I made the walker around the time Penny outgrew the crawler, so I transferred the casters from the crawler to the walker, saving the cost of another set.

What You Need

TOOLS: coping saw, saber saw or jigsaw, square, drill, screwdriver

MATERIALS:

½ in. *(12 mm)* plywood
- ☐ one piece 21 in. x 9 in. *(535 mm x 230 mm)*

1 in. x 2 in. *(17 mm x 38 mm)*
- ☐ two pieces 6 in. *(150 mm)*

quarter round
- ☐ two pieces 6 in. *(150 mm)*

- ☐ eight 1½ in. *(40 mm)* No. 8 flat-head wood screws
- ☐ carpet tacks
- ☐ Leatherette or similar cloth, approx. 20 in. x 24 in. *(500 mm x 600 mm)*
- ☐ 1 in. *(25 mm)* foam, approx. 16 in. x 21 in. *(400 mm x 535 mm)*
- ☐ four casters with 2 in. *(50 mm)* wheels with flat base (plate type, not pin type), plus ½ in. *(12 mm)* long screws for same
- ☐ strap or cloth tie

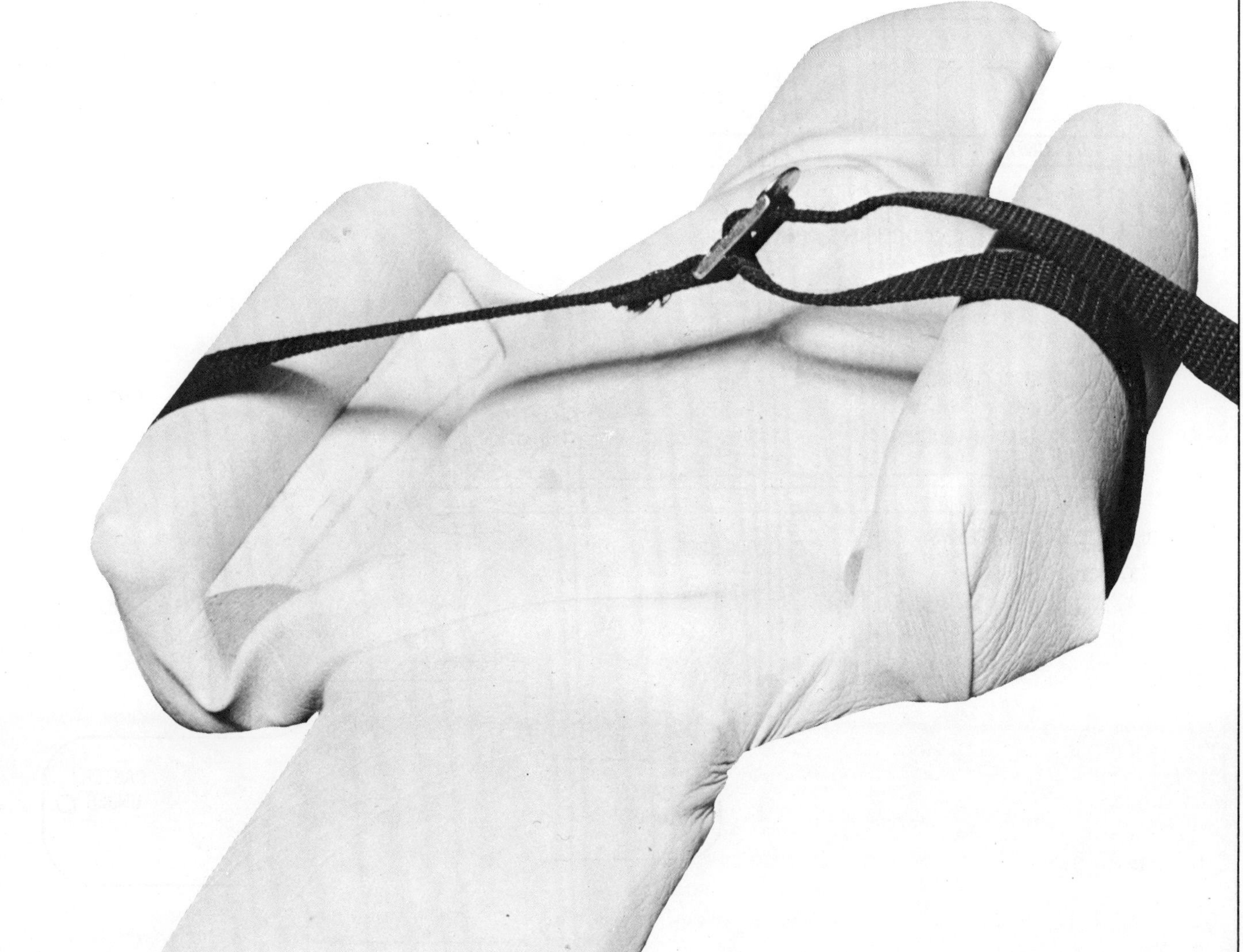

FIG. 1

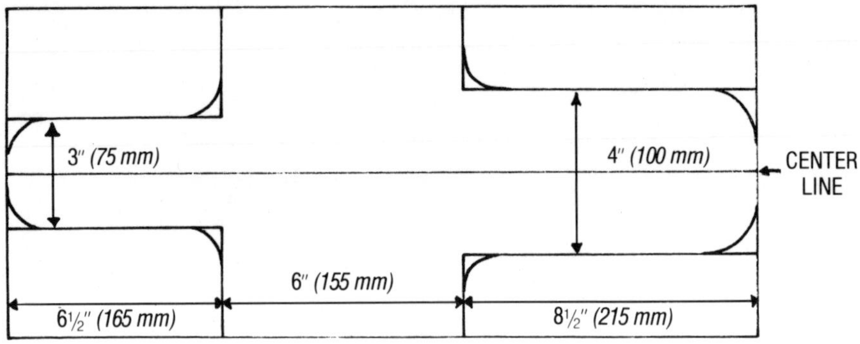

PLYWOOD SHAPE
ROUND CORNERS WHEN CUTTING

FIG. 2

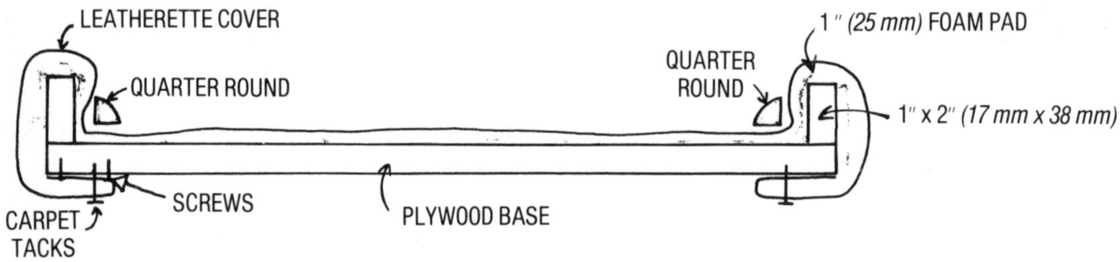

FIG. 3

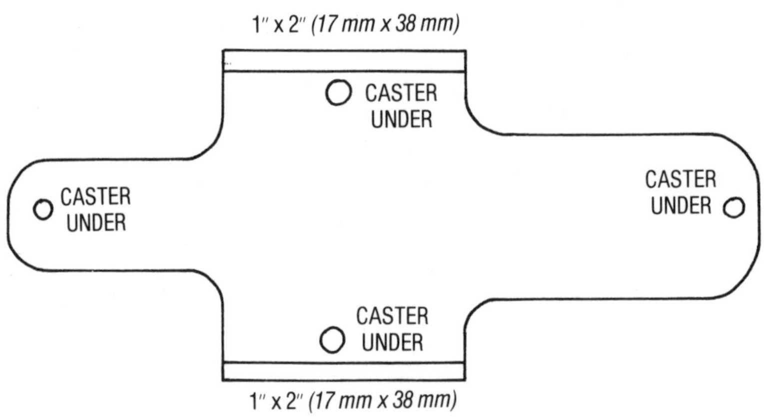

Building Instructions

Lay out the plywood and cut as in **FIGURE 1**. Round the corners as shown when cutting.

Attach the 1 in. x 2 in. *(17 mm x 38 mm)* pieces as in **FIGURE 2**, flush with the outer edges, with two screws each.

Cut the foam to fit up and over the 1 in. x 2 in. *(17 mm x 38 mm)* and across the width, from outside to outside. (See **FIGURE 2**, end view.)

Cut the Leatherette to approximately the right shape, but leave plenty of slack when attaching it, since the quarter round will go over it to pull it tight into the corner made by the plywood base and the 1 in. x 2 in. *(17 mm x 38 mm)*. Attach the pieces of quarter round with two screws each from the bottom up.

Stretch the Leatherette tight and tack into place.

Attach the casters as in **FIGURE 2**, with one near each end and at the side.

Attach a strap or cloth tie with a couple of tacks so that it fastens over the infant's back. This keeps him from sliding around while pushing on the floor.

10 Walker

At the age of five to six months a baby wants to sit up. About this time Penny became bored with always lying down, so I built a walker to help her get around.

The relatively large size of the walker allows a broad base for stability as well as a large top to help keep the baby's toys on. The piece is built from ½ in. *(12 mm)* plywood. The top is set in 1 in. *(25 mm)* from the outer edge of the bottom, not only for stability but also to protect little fingers. If the child runs the walker into the wall with his fingers over the edge, they will not be pinched.

On Penny's walker, the edge of the hole through which she sat was 9 in. *(229 mm)*—the approximate length of her arm at the time—from the edge of the top, to prevent toys from dropping over. There is no guarantee, however, that playthings will stay on the top: children do love to throw things. Since they also enjoy pounding, I covered the top of the walker with a piece of short-pile carpet to help cut down on noise.

What You Need

TOOLS: saw, square, hammer, drill and bits, screwdriver, tape measure, saber saw.
Optional: miter box to cut quarter round

MATERIALS:

½ in. *(12 mm)* plywood
- ☐ approx. one-half sheet 4 ft. x 4 ft. *(1200 mm x 1200 mm)*

1 in. x 2 in. *(17 mm x 38 mm)* pine
- ☐ two pieces 6½ in. *(165 mm)*

quarter round
- ☐ 16 linear ft. *(4800 mm)*

- ☐ four casters with 2 in. *(50 mm)* wheels for carpet (or regular), plate type, plus screws

¼ in. *(6 mm)* rope (nylon or cotton)
- ☐ two pieces 30 in. *(770 mm)* long

- ☐ short-pile carpet, 22½ in. *(570 mm)* square, for top
- ☐ two disposable diapers
- ☐ cloth for seat cover, approx. 16 in. x 12 in. *(400 mm x 305 mm)*
- ☐ No. 6 carpet tacks
- ☐ 1 in. *(25 mm)* finishing nails
- ☐ wood glue
- ☐ four 2 in. *(50 mm)* No. 6 flat-head wood screws

FIG. 1

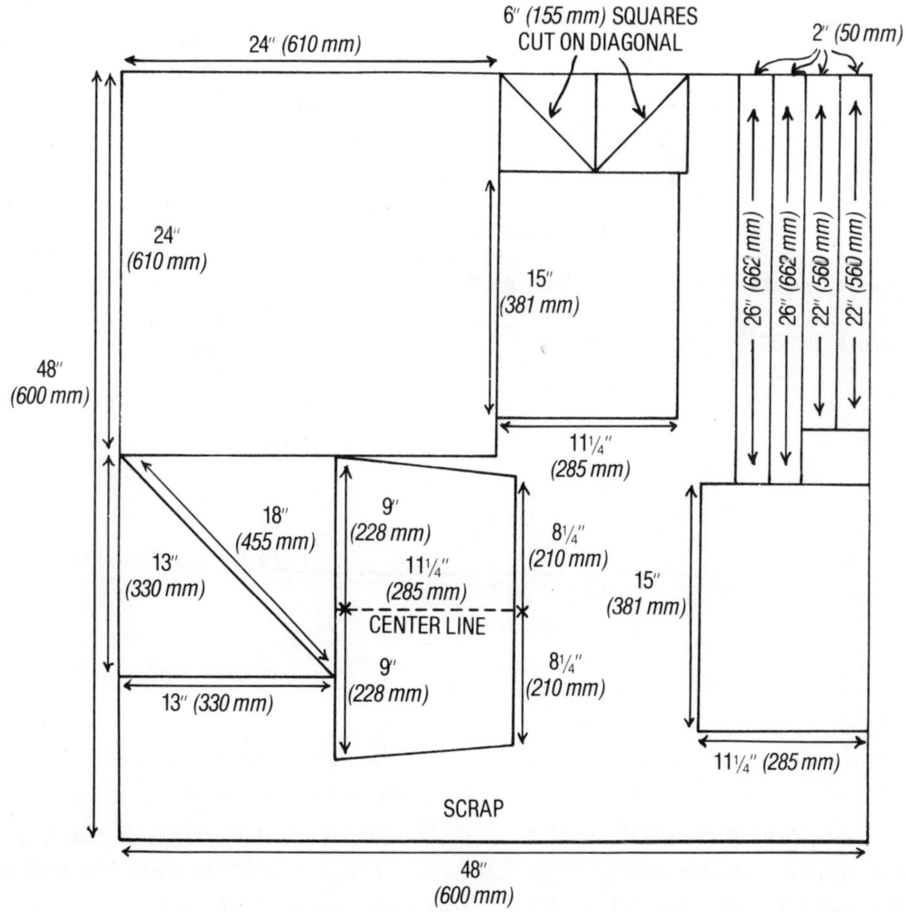

Building Instructions

Begin by cutting all the pieces of plywood as laid out in **FIGURE 1**. All cuts are straightforward except the piece for the front, which is cut on a taper. To mark this, draw a line through the center of the bottom, 9 in. *(229 mm)* from either edge, to the top. Then mark at the top, as in **FIGURE 1**, by measuring out from this centerline 8¼ in. *(210 mm)* in either direction to the upper corners. This will give the proper taper.

Lay out the base as in **FIGURE 2**, nailing and gluing the 6 in. x 6 in. *(155 mm x 155 mm)* gussets in the corners as shown. Do not put any nails right in the corners because you will be rounding these later. Be sure the frame is square by checking it with your square.

Turn the plywood over so that the gussets are on the bottom, then nail and glue the large gusset in one corner as in **FIGURE 3**. This corner will be the front; the front support will be attached to it later.

You can now round the four corners. To get a radius, simply push a 1 qt. *(or 1 l)* can into the corner until the edges of the can are flush with the edges of the plywood: mark it with a pencil, then cut the corner off using a saber saw or coping saw.

Take your time when cutting, since you are cutting through two or three layers of plywood. If a nail happens to get in the way, you will have to pull it out or somehow cut around it.

Lay out the two 11¼ in. x 15 in. *(285 mm x 380 mm)* pieces, which are the back supports. These pieces will join in the back corner as in **FIGURES 3** and **4**. Each piece will need one corner rounded to form a rounded corner where it will join the top. If the corners are not rounded they will project beyond the corner of the top. For the proper radius, use a paint can as above, and cut with your saber saw or coping saw.

Now cut a length of quarter round to go along the top and bottom of each of the two pieces, cutting the quarter-round pieces so that they roughly match the curve when placed on the inside of the upper edge. The bottom quarter-round pieces

FIG. 2

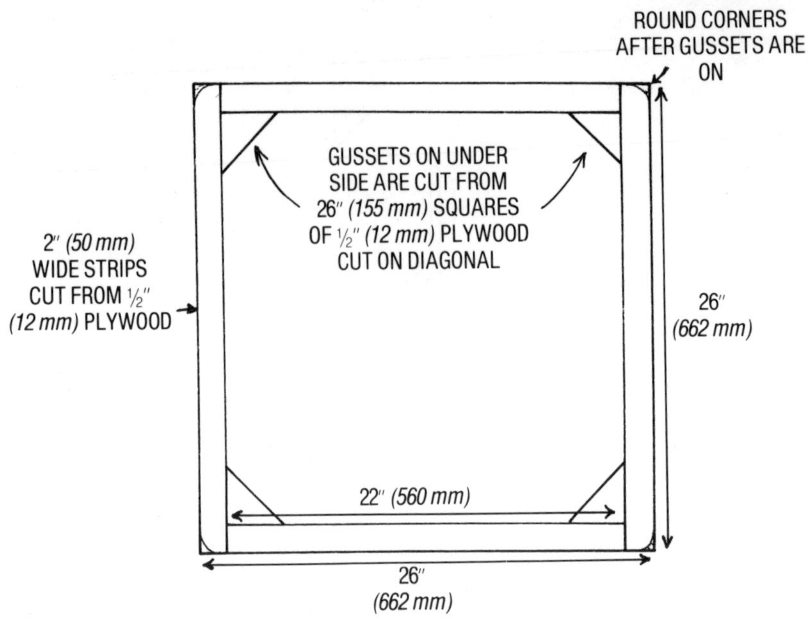

fit on the outside of these two pieces. Nail and glue them in place.

One of the two back-support pieces will need a piece of quarter round nailed on the inside edge from the bottom to the rounded corner. This will enable you to nail the two supports together to form the corner. Nail and glue this piece flush to the edge on one of the pieces. It does not matter which one, since either edge can overlap the other.

Nail and glue the two pieces together to form a corner. Try to make them square. Be sure the end of the one piece of plywood is flush with the outside edge of the other and that the bottom edges are flush. Nail down through the plywood into the quarter round.

Nail and glue the now joined pieces immediately to the bottom frame as in **FIGURES 3** and **4**. The inside edges of the support pieces should be flush with the inside edges of the bottom frame. If your corner is not exactly 90°, it can be pulled in line with the bottom frame before the glue sets.

I wanted a larger radius on the top corners, so I used a 1 gal. *(4.5 l)* paint can to mark the corners in the same manner as before. Cut off these corners with your saber saw or coping saw.

Begin working on the top by making a diagonal line from one corner to the other as in **FIGURE 5**. This line will be used to set up the circle and the seat supports. You can mark the circle with a compass, although I used a 9 in. *(229 mm)* bowl.

Check to be sure that the circle is laid out as in **FIGURE 5** by using your square to measure 9 in. *(229 mm)* from the edge of the top to your pencil mark. Drill a hole to start the cut; then cut with a saber saw or keyhole saw.

Cut and drill the 1 in. x 2 in. *(17 mm x 38 mm)* 6½ in. *(165 mm)* pieces as in **FIGURE 5**. Set them just inside the hole about ¼ in. *(6 mm)* and 90° to the diagonal centerline. Attach them with the four screws and glue. Countersink them with a ⅜ in. *(10 mm)* wood bit. Then drill the pilot and shank holes with the pieces clamped or held in place.

Take the front support piece—the one with the taper—and cut pieces of quarter round on a 45° miter to match the top and bottom length. Since these will be nailed on the outside of the piece, lay the front support on your work surface with the 18 in. *(457 mm)* side closest to you, and nail and glue the quarter rounds in place. Then nail them to the large front gusset, having the back edges of the plywood support flush with the edge of the gusset.

You are now ready to glue and nail the top on the supports. Remember that the front corner is the one with the hole in the top farthest from the corner. Place this corner over the large gusset, setting the back corner on the joined back supports. Move it around until it seems parallel to the bottom frame. There should be about ¼ in. *(6 mm)* of the top on the outside of the back support pieces.

The front support should line up, too, with the

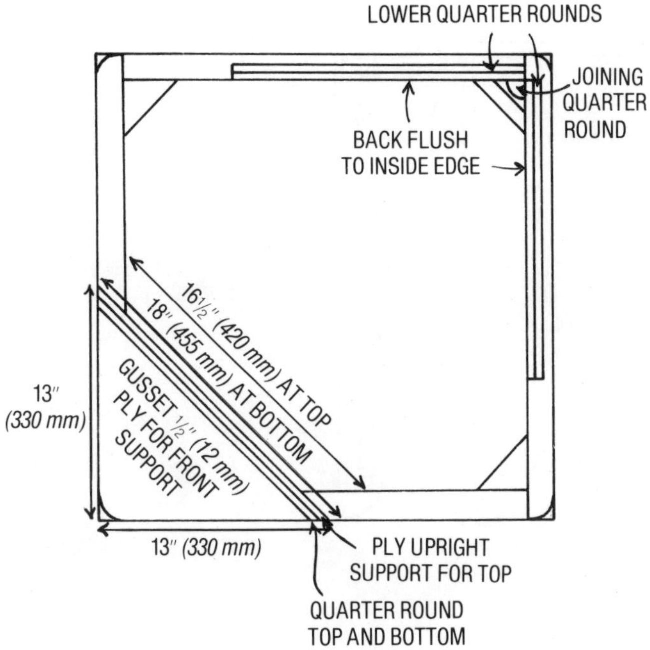

FIG. 3

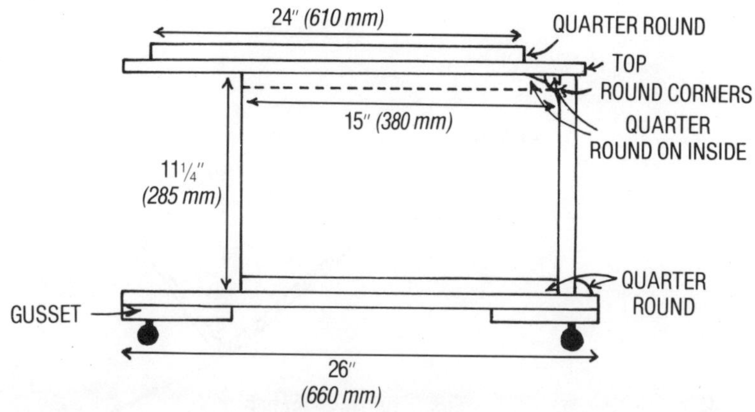

FIG. 4

upper edges just under the edges of the top. If a corner of the front support seems to stick out from under the top edge when the back is lined up, simply trim it off with your saw. When you are satisfied with the fit, glue and nail in place.

Cut pieces of quarter round 20½ in. *(520 mm)* long to go around the four edges of the top. I cut mine on a 45° miter as shown in **FIGURE 5**. The heel of the angle sticks out slightly beyond the rounded corner, but after gluing and nailing in place I smoothed it with my Surform file to match the curve. A standard file or some coarse sandpaper can also be used.

Nail and glue the quarter round to the top, the straight side flush with the outer edges of the top, leaving the smooth rounded edge on the inside. This rail helps to keep things from rolling off the top when the baby is playing. You should now sand, use your wood filler, and paint or varnish the walker.

While the paint is drying, make the seat. Take two disposable diapers and the two pieces of 30 in. *(770 mm)* rope and place the rope inside one diaper at the outer edges of the inside folds. Fold the second diaper over the first. The diapers should taper from back to front as in **FIGURE 6**.

If the diapers are more than 13 in. *(330 mm)*, cut them shorter. With the ropes in the diapers, I laid the piece on cloth (I used some old denim) about 12 in. x 16 in. *(305 mm x 410 mm)*. I tucked under the raw edges and by hand sewed a seam the length of the seat as I worked the taper in the cloth and the diapers. I then tucked the ends and raw edges under and sewed them. As I finished sewing the ends, I sewed several stitches through the cloth and through the strands of rope, to help keep everything in place.

When the walker is painted and dry, tack on the carpet using the carpet tacks, spacing them

FIG. 5

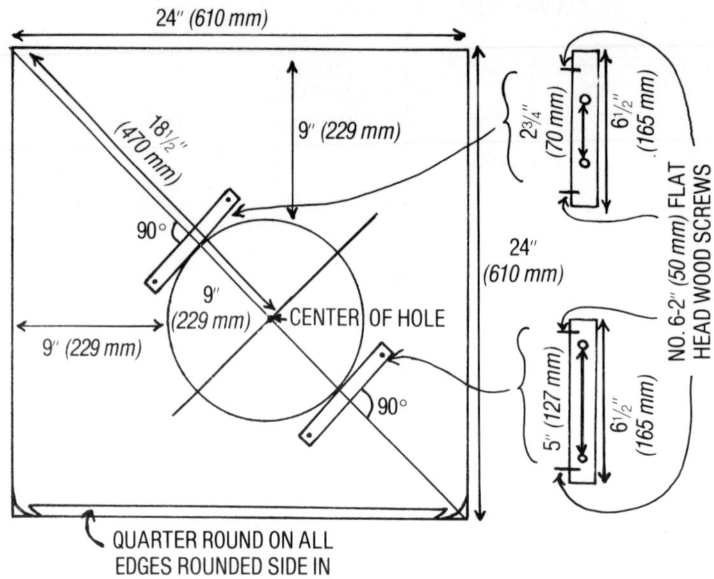

FIG. 6

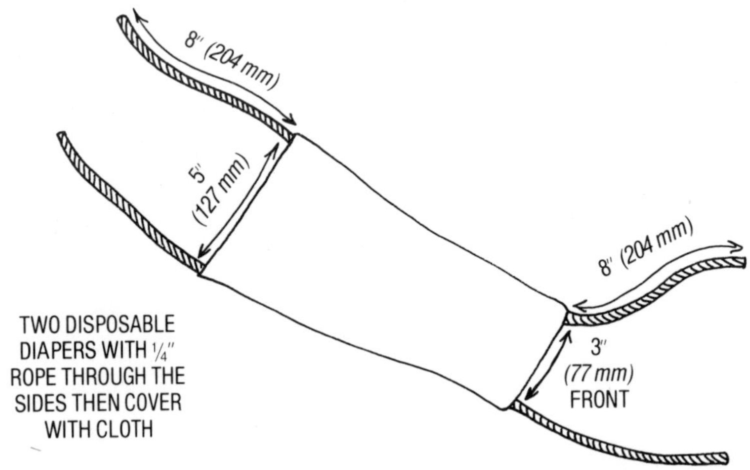

about 2 in. *(50 mm)* apart with an extra couple on the corners.

Attach the casters with screws—a ⅝ in. *(18 mm)* or ¾ in. *(20 mm)* round-head wood screw will do fine if screws do not come with the set—by drilling pilot holes for the screws and setting the casters as far to the outside of the rounded corners as possible.

Last of all, tie the seat in place by inserting the ropes through the holes, narrow end toward the front, and tying the ends together with a square knot. You may have to adjust it somewhat, but the seat right up tight to the holders suited our 27 in. *(685 mm)* baby just fine.

If your child is much taller, or grows a lot before outgrowing the use of the walker, you may want to add blocks to the underside. Simply remove the casters and cut another plywood gusset or two to raise the frame up, then set the casters on the new gussets.

Penny really loved this piece: she could sit up to do things and felt very independent.

11 Toy Box

This toy box is of medium size with carrying handles but no lid. I did not add a lid because they can be dangerous for children; a hinged lid could come crashing down on a youngster's head or fingers. Also, a child who climbs into a lidded box could become trapped inside if another child should close and sit on the lid.

A simple box such as this can have a multitude of uses around the house other than holding toys. Scale it up or down to suit your needs. It is strongly constructed and will hold heavy loads.

The box's construction is very simple and forgiving for the amateur carpenter; this is a good first project, since it goes together quickly and easily. With the corner post on the outside of the box, any crooked cuts on the end pieces are hidden. The edges of the corner posts are flush with the outer edges so that there is no possibility of error in lining up the corners, as there is when the corner posts are on the inside.

Paint the box a solid color. Then add a couple of smiling faces or other decorations in bright colors. Both you and your child will be pleased.

Use "good one side" plywood. There may be a few voids (shallow holes from knots in the surface laminate) on the inside, but these can easily be filled. You could also use more expensive "good both sides" or veneer plywood, or opt for the less expensive chipboard.

The plywood for the box can be cut from the same sheet that you use to make the indoor gym.

What You Need

TOOLS: saw, square, measuring tape, drill and ¾ in. *(20 mm)* bit, hammer

MATERIALS: ½ in. *(12 mm)* plywood, particle board or chipboard

- ☐ two pieces 30 in. x 15 in. *(762 mm x 380 mm)*
- ☐ two pieces 17 in. x 13¾ in. *(432 mm x 350 mm)*
- ☐ one piece 17 in. x 26½ in. *(432 mm x 673 mm)*

1 in. x 2 in. *(17 mm x 38 mm)* pine or fir

- ☐ four pieces 18 in. *(460 mm)*

¾ in. x ¾ in. *(17 mm x 17 mm)* pine

- ☐ two pieces 26½ in. *(673 mm)*

¾ in. *(20 mm)* hardwood dowels

- ☐ two 16⅛ in. *(410 mm)*

- ☐ 1¼ in. *(30 mm)* finishing nails

- ☐ wood glue

FIG. 1

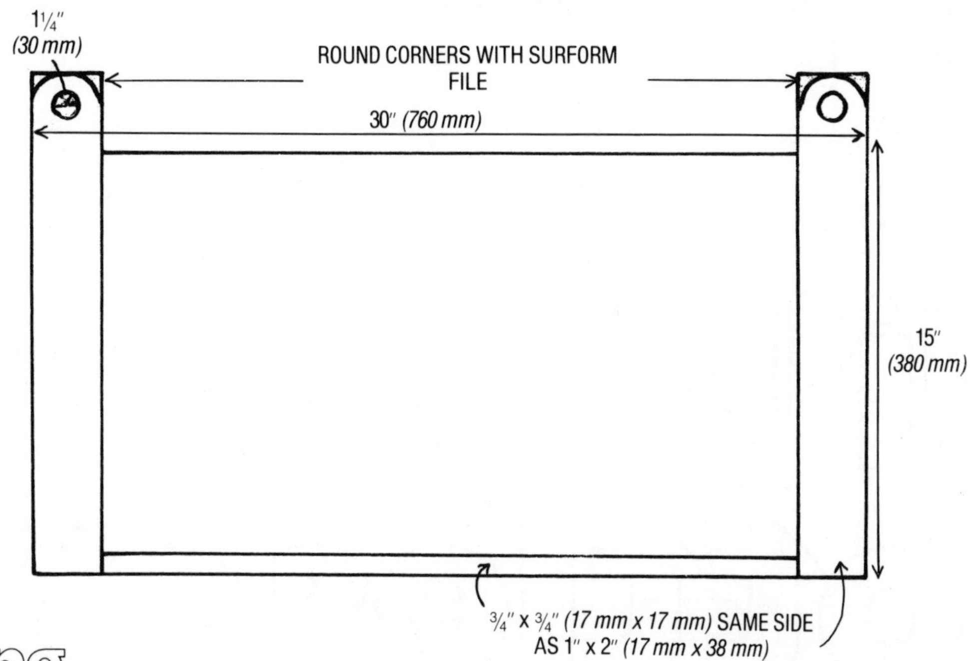

Building Instructions

Cut all pieces to size.

Drill a hole ¾ in. *(20 mm)* in diameter 1¼ in. *(32 mm)* from one end of the 1 in. x 2 in. *(17 mm x 38 mm)* pieces and centered on the width of the 1 in. x 2 in. *(17 mm x 38 mm)* as in **FIGURE 1**. Drill the hole only until the point of the drill reaches the other side. This will leave a hole about ⅜ in. *(10 mm)* deep or roughly halfway through the 1 in. x 2 in. *(17 mm x 38 mm)*.

Spread a zigzag bead of glue along the outer side (the opposite side the hole was drilled from) of the 1 in. x 2 in. *(17 mm x 38 mm)* and nail the 1 in. x 2 in. *(17 mm x 38 mm)* on the inner side of the plywood, flush along the bottom and end of the plywood as in **FIGURE 1**. Use a nail every 2 in. to 3 in. *(50 mm to 75 mm)*, nailing from each side.

In the same manner, nail and glue the ¾ in. x ¾ in. *(17 mm x 17 mm)* pieces between the upright 1 in. x 2 in. *(17 mm x 38 mm)*, having the edges flush with the bottom of the plywood.

Stand the sides up and place the bottom piece of plywood—the 17 in. x 26½ in. *(432 mm x 673 mm)*—on the ¾ in. x ¾ in. *(17 mm x 17 mm)* pieces. Fit the dowels into their holes and slip the end pieces in place on the inside edge of the 1 in. x 2 in. *(17 mm x 38 mm)*. This is a trial fit to see that all the pieces are properly cut.

Put a nail through the bottom into the ¾ in. x ¾ in. *(17 mm x 17 mm)* at about the middle to hold it in place.

Tip the box on one end and spread glue along the inside edge of the corner posts. Place one end piece of plywood in its place. With a helper holding the sides tightly together at that end, also with the dowels in place, nail the plywood to the corner posts.

Tip the box on the other end and repeat the above procedure.

Your box is complete, but you will notice that when you pick it up by the handles, they roll. Prevent this by setting a nail in from the edge of the corner posts into the dowels.

If you should happen to break one of the handles, drill through from the outside edge of one of the corner posts and slide in a new handle from that side.

Another modification you might like is to add casters. Use the pin type, and drill the hole for them offset toward the plywood in the bottom of the corner posts.

If you do want a lid for the box, I recommend that you cut a piece of ½ in. *(12 mm)* plywood to fit flush with the outer edges of the sides and ends, then glue and nail some ¾ in. x ¾ in. *(17 mm x 17 mm)* to the underside ⅝ in. *(16 mm)* in from the edges to keep it in place. Thus, if the top is opened, it must be removed.

To keep the top near the box you might tie a rope ¼ in. *(6 mm)* in diameter to one of the handle supports, then lead the end through a hole drilled through the lid with a stopper knot on the underside.

12

Milk Bottles

Toddlers love things that they can manipulate "just like grown-ups." I made Penny this set of milk bottles at about one year of age, and she was fascinated by them. She would take each milk bottle out, then carefully place it back in the holder again. This type of activity is very good for developing hand-eye coordination.

Later she would put things in plastic cups that fit the holes and carry them around. She would even carry her things toward the door, saying "bye-bye" as if taking her work to the office.

The carrier is easily made out of leftovers from other projects. The 1½ in. *(40 mm)* pine doweling that I used was left over from a stairwell handrail.

What You Need

TOOLS: saw, miter box, drill and hole saw, ¾ in. *(18 mm)* bit, hammer, Surform file, coping or saber saw

MATERIALS:

¼ in. *(6 mm)* plywood
- ☐ two pieces 7¼ in. x 8½ in. *(186 mm x 218 mm)*
- ☐ one piece 2½ in. x 4½ in. *(64 mm x 115 mm)*

1 in. *(17 mm)* softwood
- ☐ enough to make two pieces 2¼ in. x 7¼ in. *(55 mm x 186 mm)*

quarter round
- ☐ two pieces 4½ in. *(115 mm)*

1½ in. *(40 mm)* softwood dowel
- ☐ one 27 in. *(690 mm)* or enough to make six 4½ in. *(115 mm)* bottles

- ☐ ¾ in. *(20 mm)* finishing nails
- ☐ glue

FIG. 1

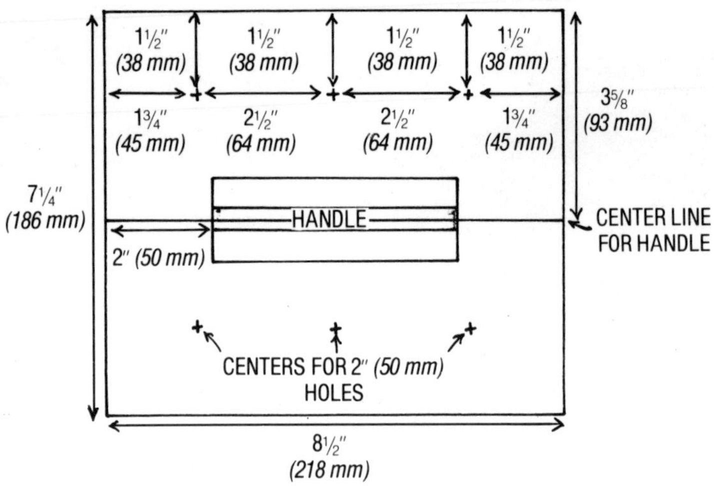

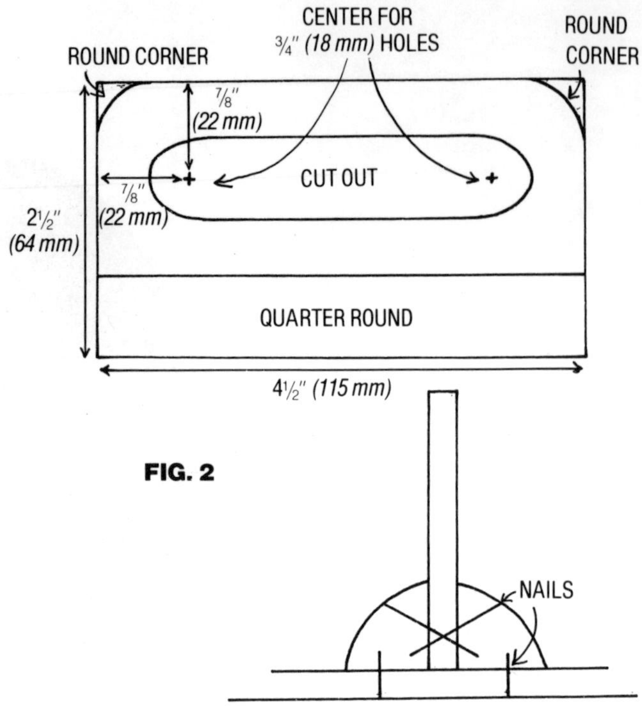

FIG. 2

FIG. 3

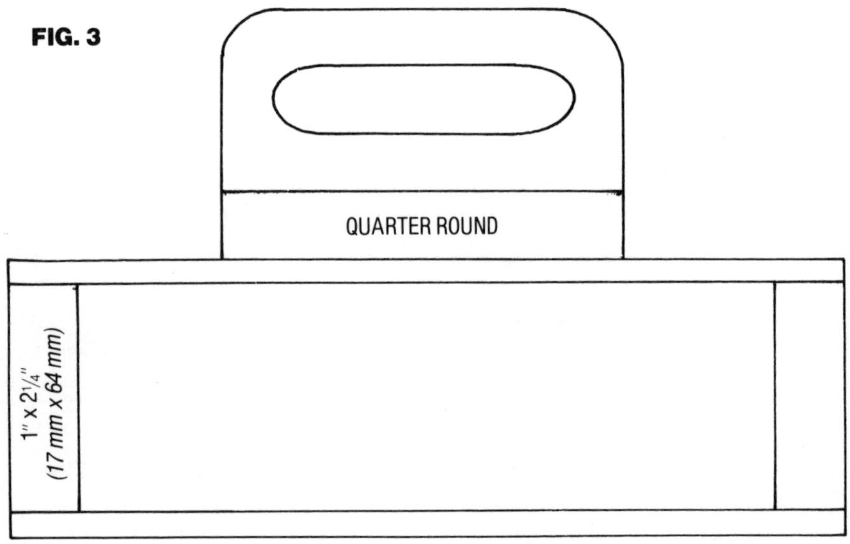

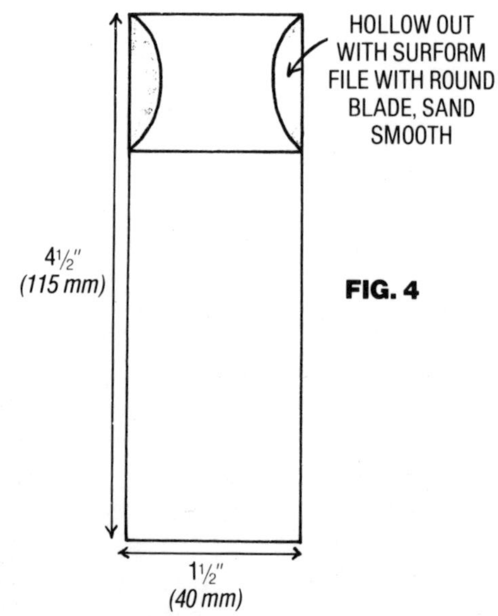

FIG. 4

MAKE 6, OR USE PLASTIC CUPS OR YOGURT CUPS

Building Instructions

Cut out the three pieces of ¼ in. *(6 mm)* plywood and lay out one of the 7¼ in. x 8½ in. *(186 mm x 218 mm)* pieces as in **FIGURE 1**. Using your drill and hole saw, cut out the 2 in. *(50 mm)* holes.

Lay out the piece for the handle, drill the ¾ in. *(18 mm)* holes as indicated in **FIGURE 2**, and cut out between the holes with a coping or saber saw.

Assemble the handle as shown in **FIGURE 2**, and glue and nail it to the plywood piece with the holes as shown in **FIGURE 1**.

Rip out the 2¼ in. x 7¼ in. *(55 mm x 186 mm)* softwood pieces. I ripped them out of a 1 in. x 6 in. *(17 mm x 140 mm)* piece of pine. Glue and nail the pieces together as in **FIGURE 3**.

Cut the dowel to length and shape it as in **FIGURE 4**, using a round-bladed Surform file. Since I did this by hand, my pieces are not perfectly symmetrical all the way around but are certainly adequate. Sand with medium sandpaper to smooth the marks from the Surform file.

For a finish I sanded everything smooth and then applied a coat of sanding sealer. I sanded lightly again after the wood was dry.

13

Pushing Cart

A child beginning to walk needs something to lean against to give him confidence in maintaining his balance. The pushing cart has a bar to hold onto, set over the rear wheels so that the cart will not tip over backward onto the toddler as he puts his weight against it. When the child learns to walk, the cart will become his favorite plaything. As he gets older he will continue to enjoy giving his toys a ride.

This item is a nice toy that can be made in an afternoon, and a store-bought substitute is difficult to find. It is built for heavy use and abuse. The plywood wheels are easily made with a wing cutter.

What You Need

TOOLS: saw, square, hammer, tape measure, drill and bits, wing cutter and screwdriver.

MATERIALS:

½ in. *(12 mm)* plywood
- ☐ one piece 9 in. x 16½ in. *(228 mm x 420 mm)*
- ☐ two pieces 10 in. x 18 in. *(253 mm x 457 mm)*
- ☐ two pieces 9 in. x 8¾ in. *(228 mm x 222 mm)*
- ☐ scrap to cut four 4 in. *(102 mm)* in diameter wheels

¾ in. x ¾ in. *(17 mm x 17 mm)*
- ☐ two pieces 16½ in. *(420 mm)*
- ☐ four pieces 10 in. *(254 mm)*

1 in. x 2 in. *(17 mm x 38 mm)*
- ☐ two pieces 20 in. *(508 mm)*

- ☐ ¾ in. *(20 mm)* dowel, 10½ in. *(267 mm)*
- ☐ four 1½ in. *(38 mm)* No. 10 round-head wood screws, with eight flat washers for same
- ☐ 1 in. *(25 mm)* finishing nails
- ☐ glue

FIG. 1

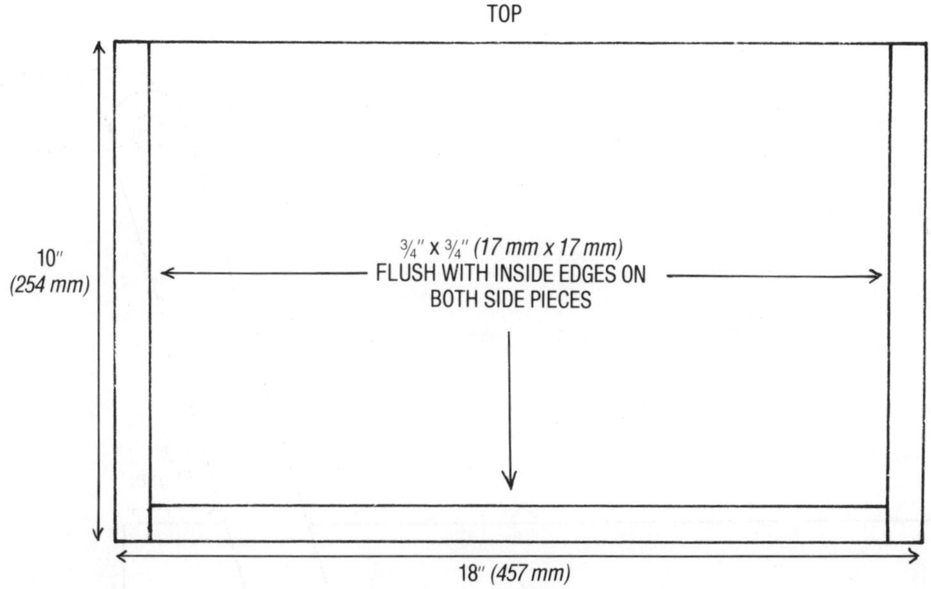

FIG. 2

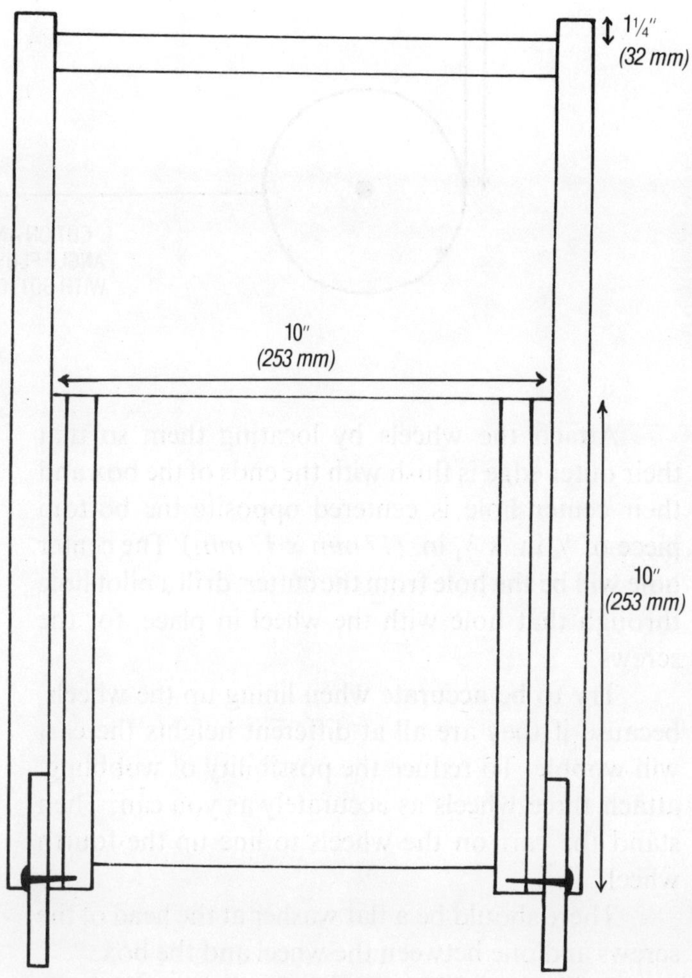

Building Instructions

Cut the plywood and ¾ in. x ¾ in. *(17 mm x 17 mm)* to size. Glue and nail the ¾ in. x ¾ in. *(17 mm x 17 mm)* to the inner side of the side pieces as in **FIGURE 1**.

Hold the two sides parallel to each other and place the bottom piece on the bottom ¾ in. x ¾ in. *(17 mm x 17 mm)*. This will line up the sides. Put one of the end pieces in place; tip the pieces so that they are standing on that end. When the bottom piece is in position, glue and nail the end piece in place.

Lay the piece on its bottom and glue and nail the bottom in place. Put in the other end and glue and nail that piece in place.

Cut the four wheels using your drill and wing cutter. I made the wheels 4 in. *(102 mm)* in diameter. The cutter on the sliding wing will have one position for cutting holes, with the rough edge on the inner side of the circle. By reversing or turning the cutter over, the smooth side will be on the outside of the cut. This is the proper position for cutting wheels. Make a trial cut before making the wheels.

FIG. 3

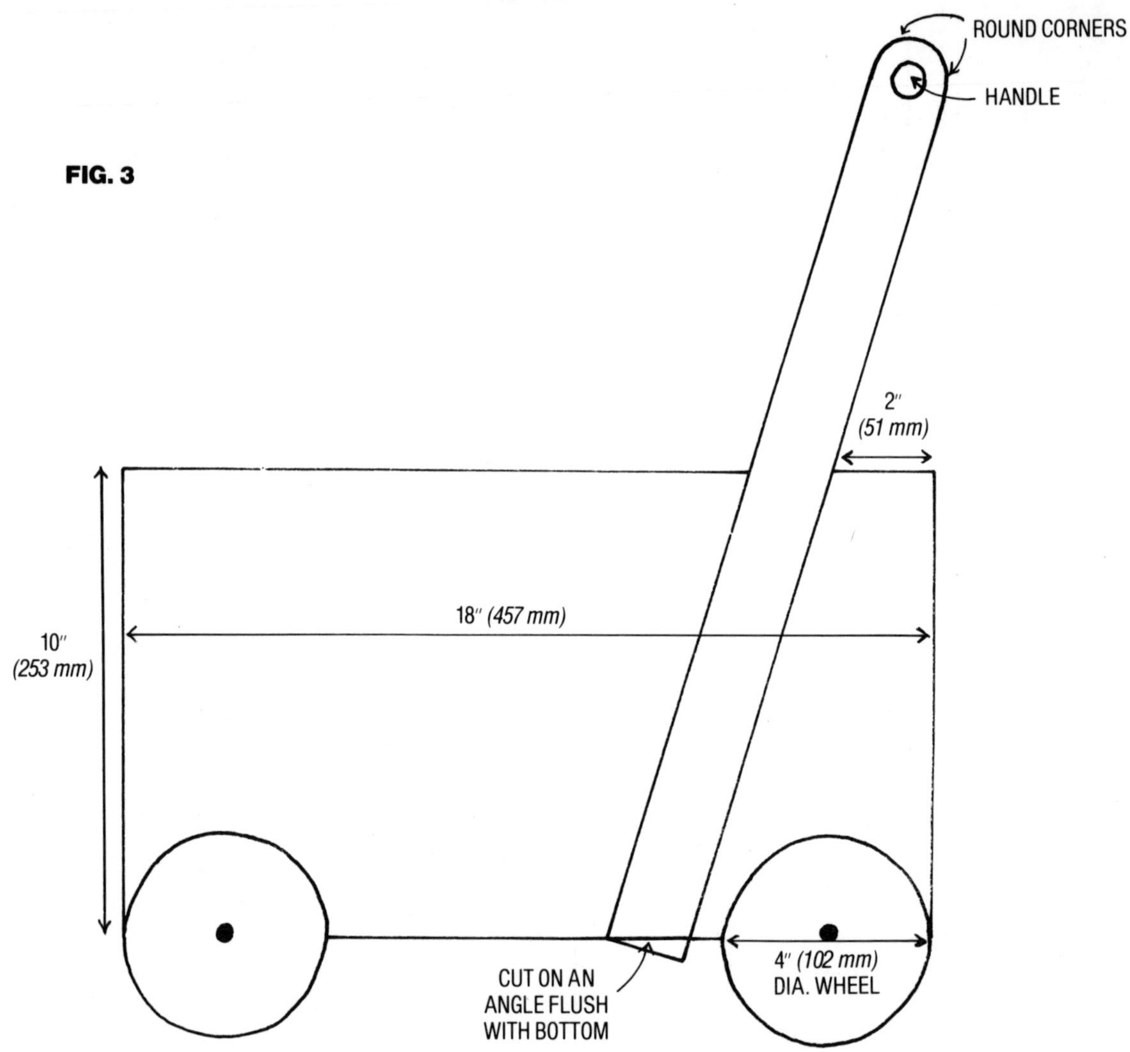

Attach the wheels by locating them so that their outer edge is flush with the ends of the box and their center hole is centered opposite the bottom piece of ¾ in. x ¾ in. *(17 mm x 17 mm).* The center hole will be the hole from the cutter: drill a pilot hole through that hole with the wheel in place, for the screws.

Try to be accurate when lining up the wheels, because if they are all at different heights the cart will wobble. To reduce the possibility of wobbling, attach three wheels as accurately as you can. Then stand the cart on the wheels to line up the fourth wheel.

There should be a flat washer at the head of the screws and one between the wheel and the box.

Drill a ¾ in. *(20 mm)* hole for the dowel handle 1¼ in. *(32 mm)* from one end of each of the 1 in. x 2 in. *(17 mm x 38 mm).* Drill the hole only halfway through the 1 in. x 2 in. *(17 mm x 38 mm)* or until the point of your drill bit just begins to break through the wood. Cut the dowel to length, then attach the 1 in. x 2 in. *(17 mm x 38 mm)* as in FIGURE 3, with the bottom end ½ in. *(12 mm)* forward of the rear wheels. Set some nails from the inside of the box through the plywood into the 1 in. x 2 in. *(17 mm x 38 mm).* Be sure you have the dowel in place before the second 1 in. x 2 in. *(17 mm x 38 mm)* is attached.

Set a nail in from the edge of the 1 in. x 2 in. *(17 mm x 38 mm)* to prevent the handle from rolling.

14

Step·up

The step-up is another multipurpose item that can be useful to both children and adults. At only 12 in. *(305 mm)* high with a 6 in. *(152 mm)* step, it enables the small child to get up high enough to wash hands at the sink, help do the dishes and also, I suppose, get into mischief by making more things within reach. It can be a handy stool or even a work top for doing drawings on when sitting on the floor.

Even though the step-up is only 12 in. *(305 mm)* high, we adults sometimes need just that much extra height to reach the top shelf in the kitchen cupboards or at the back of the closet. It is strong enough for any human weight, yet its plywood construction makes it very light.

By eighteen months Penny came to regard the step-up as her personal possession. She moved it all over the kitchen to get to counter height and found great pleasure in "helping" (watching) Fiona chop vegetables or mix cakes.

To reduce the boxlike appearance I cut out the shape of a duck in the back panel. You could do likewise, or just paint a design or stick on a decal.

As you can see, the step-up is of very simple construction and can be made easily and quickly.

What You Need

TOOLS: saw, hammer, square, tape measure, drill and ½ in. *(12 mm)* and ⅝ in. *(16 mm)* bits. *Optional: miter box for cutting quarter round*

MATERIALS:

- ☐ ½ in. *(12 mm)* plywood, 25 in. x 34 in. *(640 mm x 870 mm)*
- ☐ ½ in. *(12 mm)* dowel, 12 in. *(305 mm)*
- ☐ 4 ft. *(1250 mm)* quarter round
- ☐ 1 in. *(25 mm)* finishing nails
- ☐ glue

FIG. 1

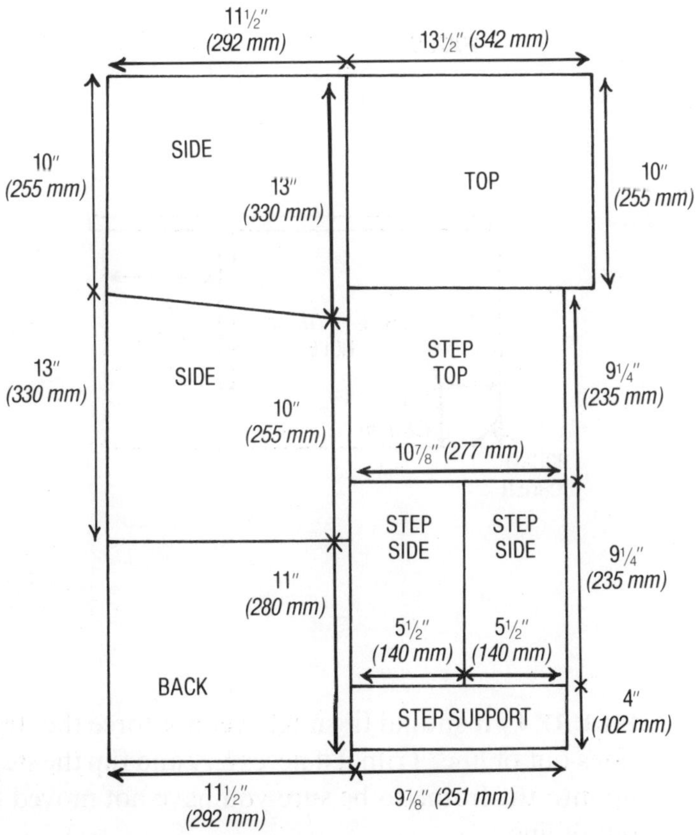

FIG. 2

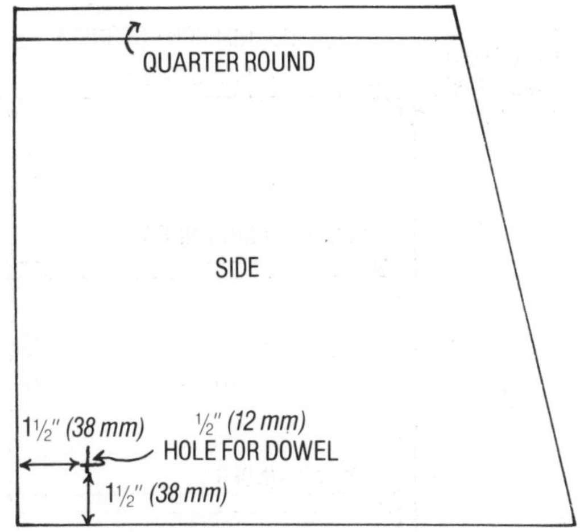

FIG. 3

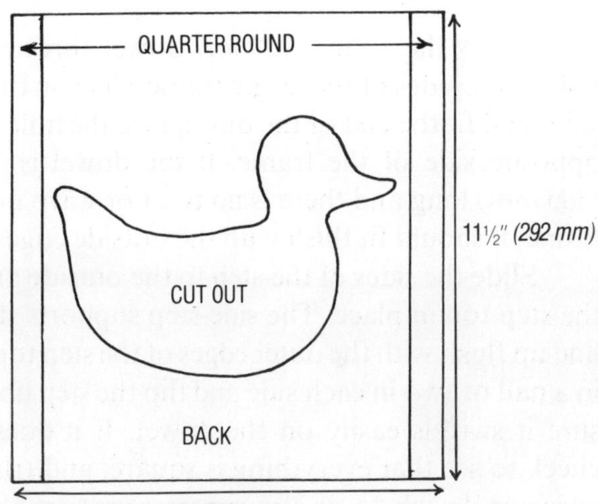

Building Instructions

Begin by laying out the plywood as in **FIGURE 1**, and cut all pieces.

Glue and nail a piece of quarter round along the top of each side piece. Since the quarter round must be at the top of the outer side of the side pieces, stand them up in the final assembled position to be sure you have them on the proper side.

Drill a ½ in. *(12 mm)* hole for the dowel in each side as indicated in **FIGURE 2**. The center of the hole is 1½ in. *(38 mm)* from the front edge, and 1½ in. *(38 mm)* up from the bottom edge on both sides.

Cut pieces of quarter round to fit at the side edges of the back piece, then glue and nail them on flush with the 11½ in. *(292 mm)* edges. (See **FIGURE 3**.) If you intend to cut out an animal or other shape in the back piece, do so now before the unit is assembled. If you are cutting out the shape, it will be easier to cut with a saber saw from the side opposite the side to which the quarter round is attached.

Glue and nail the side pieces to the back piece, but be sure the bottom edges are flush and that the pieces of quarter round on the back pieces are flush with the outside back edges of the side pieces.

You can now nail and glue on the top of the step-up. The quarter round on the side pieces should line up and be flush with the outside edges of the top. Nail around the top into both the quarter round and the plywood at the back.

Take the step top and pass it through the front of the frame that you just nailed together, to see if it will fit easily. It may need to be trimmed slightly with your saw or plane. A clearance of ⅛ in. *(3 mm)* or so is enough.

Drill a ⅝ in. *(16 mm)* hole in each side-step support as indicated in **FIGURE 5**, with the hole centered 1½ in. *(38 mm)* from the bottom and from the back edge.

FIG. 4

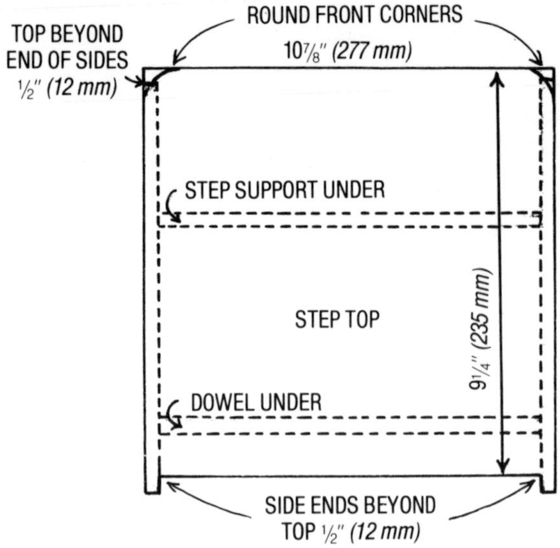

FIG. 5

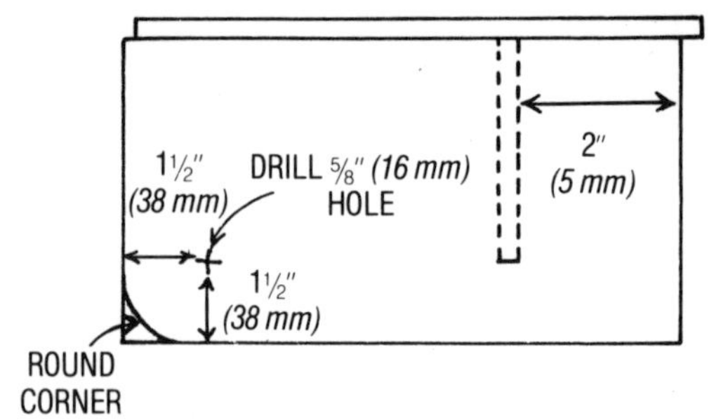

Insert the ½ in. *(12 mm)* dowel through the hole in the sides of the larger frame, slide on the step sides and fit the end of the dowel into the hole in the opposite side of the frame. If the dowel is 12 in. *(305 mm)* long and there is no twist or warp in your frame, it should fit flush with the outside edges.

Slide the sides of the step to the outside and set the step top in place. The side-step supports should line up flush with the outer edges of the step top. Put in a nail or two in each side and flip the step up to be sure it swivels easily on the dowel. If it does not, check to see that everything is square, and trim the edges or do whatever else is necessary to make the step hinge easily up into the larger frame.

When everything fits well, glue and nail the step top to the step sides. Turning the large frame onto its front with the step top lying flat on your work surface, put the step support between the step sides, fitting it up to the underside of the step top and to the inside edges of the step sides. (See FIGURE 4.) It should fit snugly yet not force the step sides out of line. Trim it if necessary and flip the step up into the frame to be sure you have not moved it out of line.

Glue and nail this piece, first from the outside of the step sides. Then put some nails through the top into the support.

You are nearly done, and your step-up should look complete. When you lift the step-up off the floor you will notice that as the step is flipped back inside the large frame, the step top knocks against the back piece. Since I found this annoying, I took a piece of quarter round about 3 in. *(75 mm)* long and glued and nailed it to the inside of one of the side pieces. In its up position the step lies against this piece of quarter round and does not fall against the back piece when lifted off the floor.

Fill the voids and nail holes with wood filler, then sand and paint.

15

Booster Seat

If you like to make small handy items for your child, there seems to be a never ending list of worthwhile projects.

When Penny was about twenty-one months old, she, her mother and I began to get tired of the high chair. Fiona asked me to make a booster chair, and this is what I produced the following afternoon. As you can see, it is very simple but suits the purpose admirably.

I made it to fit in a large wooden chair with arms. If you don't need such a wide and deep booster chair, just scale it down. The sides should be at least 2 in. *(50 mm)* from the edge of the chair on either side, with the front edge of the booster seat just in from the front of the edge of the chair.

I made Penny's booster seat from some left-over ½ in. *(12 mm)* particle board. Any plywood of similar thickness would do as well.

What You Need

TOOLS: saw, hammer, drill and bits, screwdriver, saber saw or coping saw

MATERIALS: ½ in. *(12 mm)* particle board or plywood

- ☐ one piece 22 in. x 30 in. *(510 mm x 760 mm)*

¾ in. x ¾ in. *(17 mm x 17 mm)*

- ☐ one piece 36 in. *(915 mm)*
- ☐ 1 in. *(25 mm)* finishing nails
- ☐ twelve 1 in. *(25 mm)* No. 6 flat-head wood screws

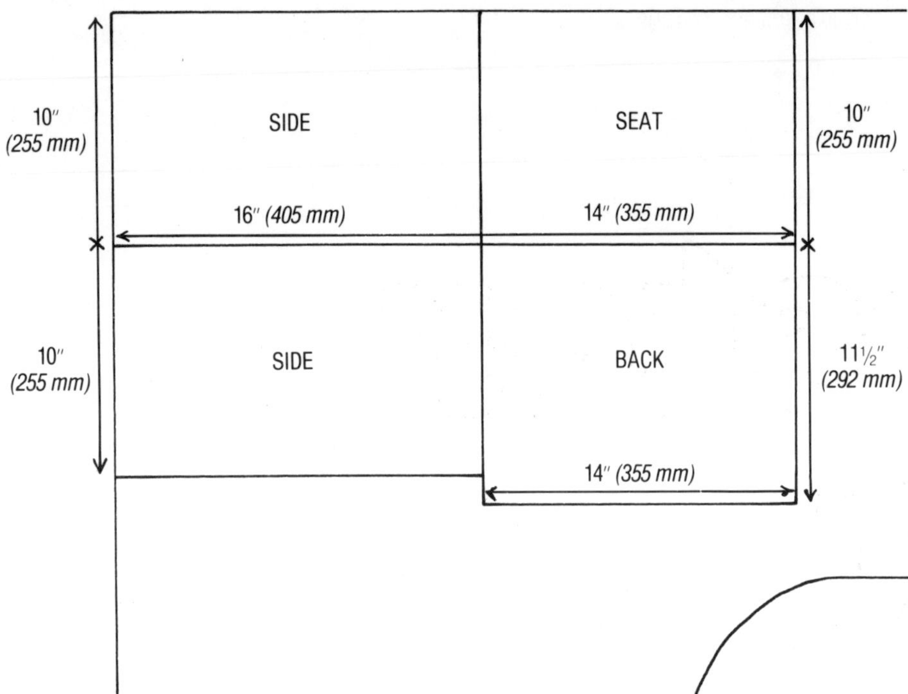

FIG. 1

FIG. 2

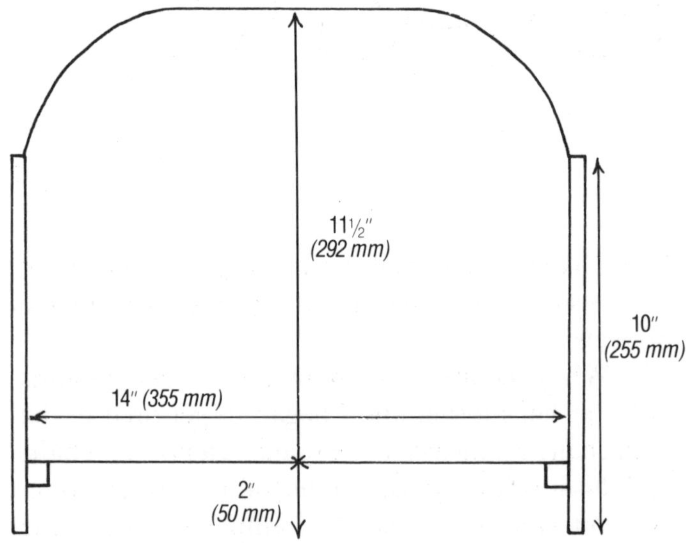

Building Instructions

Cut out the four main pieces. (See **FIGURE 1**.) Then round the corners as shown in **FIGURES 2** and **3**, including the top corners of the back and the front of the side pieces.

Cut two pieces of the ¾ in. x ¾ in. *(17 mm x 17 mm)* 10 in. *(255 mm)* long, then nail and glue these to the bottom of the side edges of the seat, flush with the edges.

Make a pencil mark along the inside of the sides 2½ in. *(63 mm)* from the bottom. This will be the height of the top edge of the seat. Drill the holes and set two screws each side into the ¾ in. x ¾ in. *(17 mm x 17 mm)* from the outside.

Attach two pieces of the ¾ in. x ¾ in. *(17 mm x 17 mm)* to the back along the sides, as with the seat. The ends should be flush with the bottom, not the top. Slide the back in place at the angle indicated in **FIGURE 3**, and fix with two screws on each side. Since the lower edge of the back should overlap the back edge of the seat, a few nails can be driven through the back piece into the seat.

Fill the nail and screw holes with wood filler and fill any gaps around the seat and back. I gave Penny's booster seat one undercoat, then two coats of white semigloss enamel.

15—Fig 3

FIG. 3

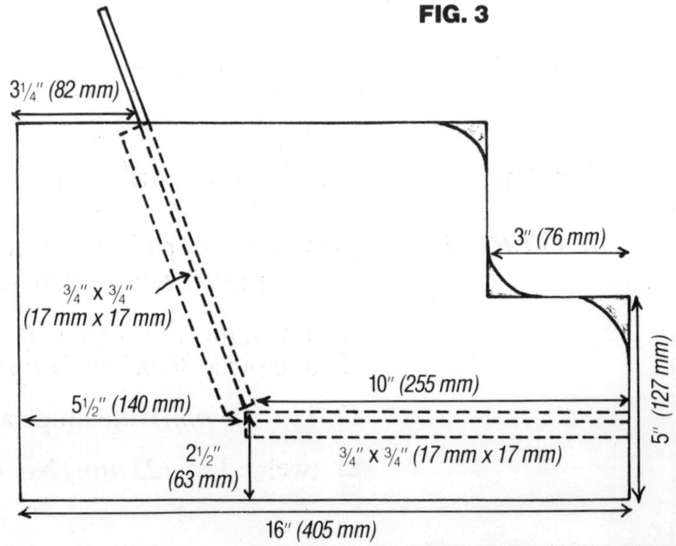

16

Zooms

I made my first zoom, the easiest toy on wheels, in about half an hour with an anxious four-year-old at my side asking a constant stream of questions. He could hardly wait to see what his new toy would look like. I was somewhat less anxious, but was equally satisfied with the final result.

What You Need

TOOLS: saw, square, hole saw, drill and ¾ in. *(18 mm)* and ⅞ in. *(22 mm)* bits, hammer, coping saw or jigsaw

MATERIALS:

¾ in. *(18 mm)* dowels
- ☐ one approx. 3½ in. *(89 mm)*
- ☐ two 2 in. *(50 mm)*

2 in. x 4 in. *(38 mm x 89 mm)* pine or fir
- ☐ one piece 10 in. *(255 mm)*

1 in. x 2 in. *(17 mm x 38 mm)* pine or fir
- ☐ two pieces 4¾ in. *(120 mm)*

2 in. x 2 in. *(38 mm x 38 mm)* pine
- ☐ one piece 6 in. *(150 mm)*

½ in. *(12 mm)* plywood
- ☐ scrap to make three wheels 2¼ in. *(57 mm)* in diameter

- ☐ glue

- ☐ 1¼ in. *(32 mm)* finishing nails

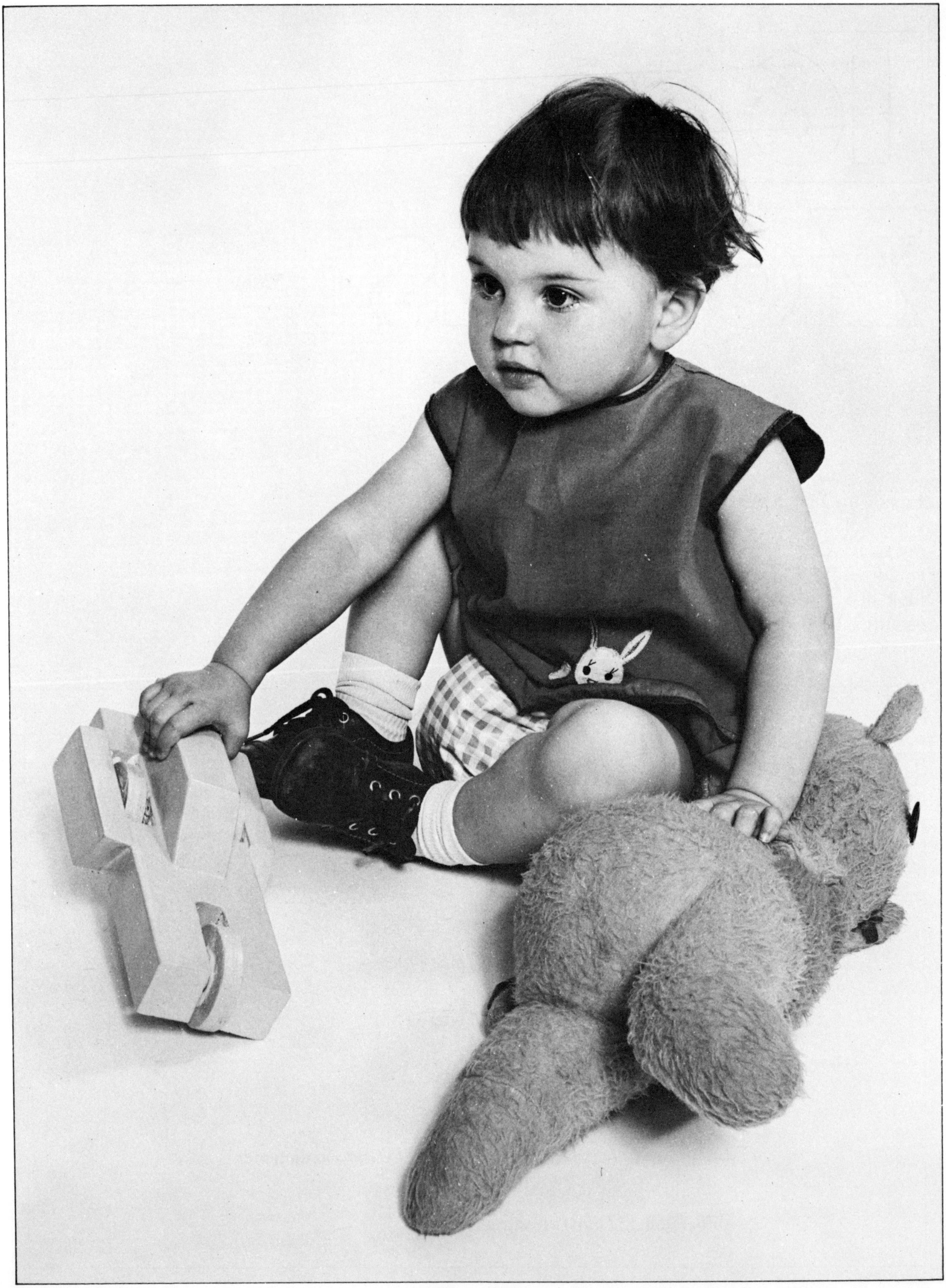

FIG. 1

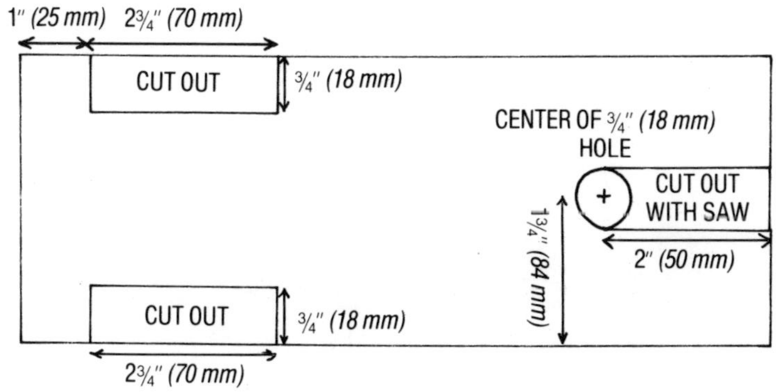

FIG. 2

FIG. 3

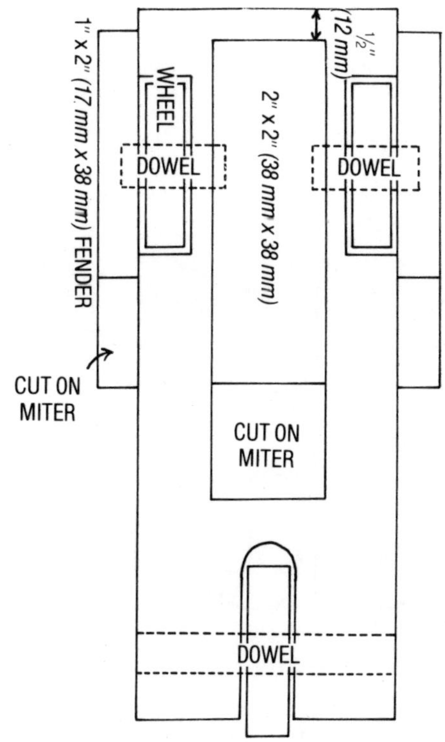

Building Instructions

Begin by drilling a hole ¾ in. *(18 mm)* in diameter 2 in. *(50 mm)* in from the front end of the zoom, centered on the width. Then make the parallel cuts to join that hole to the end. (See **FIGURE 1**.)

Make the side notches for the wheels as in **FIGURE 1**. Make the inside cuts using your coping saw or jigsaw. Cut the 1 in. x 2 in. *(17 mm x 38 mm)* to length, but remember that these are the fenders and could be shaped with the ends rounded or angled for a more stylish appearance.

Drill the holes for the dowels using the ¾ in. *(18 mm)* drill bit. Drill a hole all the way through the front forks for the front wheel. (See **FIGURE 2**.) For the side wheels, drill halfway through the 1 in. x 2 in. *(17 mm x 38 mm)*. Then drill the holes for the dowels into the side of the 2 in. x 4 in. *(38 mm x 89 mm)* 2⅜ in. *(60 mm)* from the end, and half of its thickness. Drill these holes only about ¾ in. *(18 mm)* deep.

To make the wheels, use the 2¼ in. *(57 mm)* cutter for your hole saw. Drill out the wheels, making three of them. You now have wheels with ¼ in. *(6 mm)* holes that need to be drilled to ⅞ in. *(22 mm)*. Put the wheels in a clamp: if you do not have good clamps, you can temporarily nail the wheels down to a piece of wood using your 1¼ in. *(32 mm)* finishing nails. Drill the holes, then pull out the nails. The nail holes can be filled with wood filler or can just be left in the wood.

If you are going to paint the zoom, you may want to do so before it is assembled, since the paint could make the wheels stick if it runs down between the dowels and the wheels.

Assemble the zoom by putting a wheel in the forks, then pushing through the dowel. A dab of glue or a nail from the top into the dowel will hold it in place. Assemble the side wheels by inserting the dowel in the hole, slide on a wheel, then line up the hole and dowel on the 1 in. x 2 in. *(17 mm x 38 mm)*. A dab of glue on the 1 in. x 2 in. *(17 mm x 38 mm)* where it goes against the 2 in. x 4 in. *(38 mm x 89 mm)* will ensure that it stays there. You will notice that the zoom runs on its wheels on either side.

As an extra feature you might add a block that measures 2 in. x 2 in. *(38 mm x 38 mm)* 6 in. *(150 mm)* long, behind the front wheel between the rear wheels, for a pushing handle. This can be glued in place.

If your child is less than two years old, he will like to pull things behind him. Attach a string by pounding a staple into the wood behind the front wheel. Put a block under the zoom to keep the wheels off the floor when pounding, otherwise you may split them.

17

Stacking Cubes

When Penny was walking and exploring the house at about one year of age, she enjoyed these cubes for their light weight. They were handy for sitting and standing on, as well as for stacking. She could easily lift or push them; that she was able to handle such big things seemed to delight her. And she was very pleased to discover that the blocks gave her access to objects normally out of reach!

Penny's friends, including children up to six years old, played with the cubes in many different ways. The pecking order was revealed in who got the largest block to sit on.

The cubes are made from light wall paneling. Mine were made with some leftovers from a remodeling job. The plywood should be flush on the outside; if you have some paneling with grooves running up it, use the grooved side for the inside.

A piece of paneling 24 in. x 48 in. *(600 mm x 1200 mm)* will make a set of three cubes: one 8 in. *(200 mm)*, one 7 in. *(180 mm)* and one 6 in. *(150 mm)*. All the cubes are made the same way.

What You Need

TOOLS: saw, miter box, square, measuring tape, hammer

MATERIALS:

3/16 in. *(4 mm)* plywood paneling

- ☐ one piece 24 in. x 48 in. *(600 mm x 1200 mm)*

1/2 in. x 1/2 in. *(12 mm x 12 mm)* molding, sometimes called plate stop. Other moldings such as 3/4 in. x 3/4 in. *(17 mm x 17 mm)* quarter round could also be used.

- ☐ 20 linear ft. *(6 m)*
- ☐ 5/8 in. *(16 mm)* finishing nails
- ☐ glue

FIG. 1

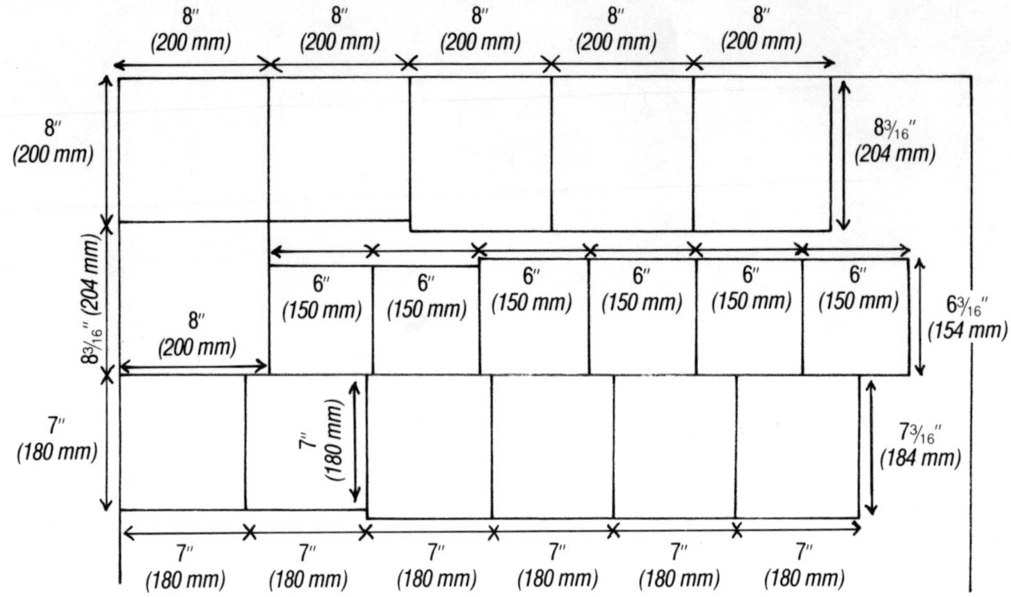

FIG. 2

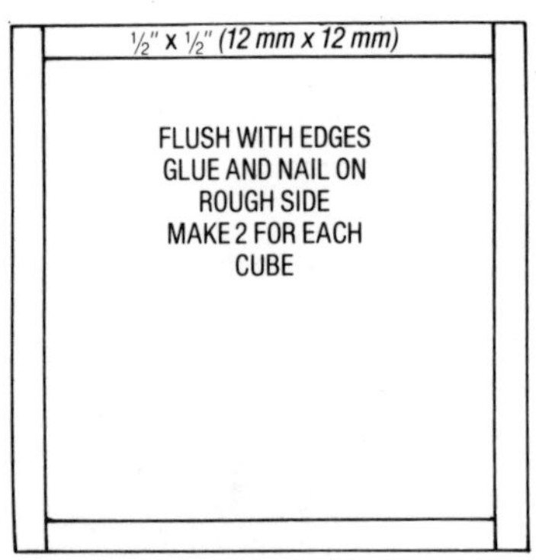

FIG. 3

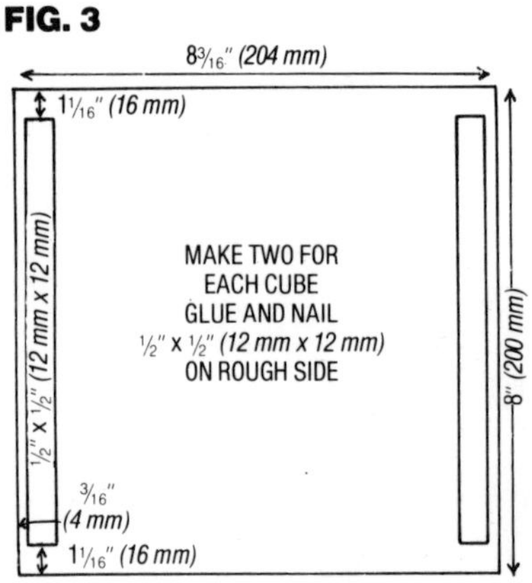

FIG. 4

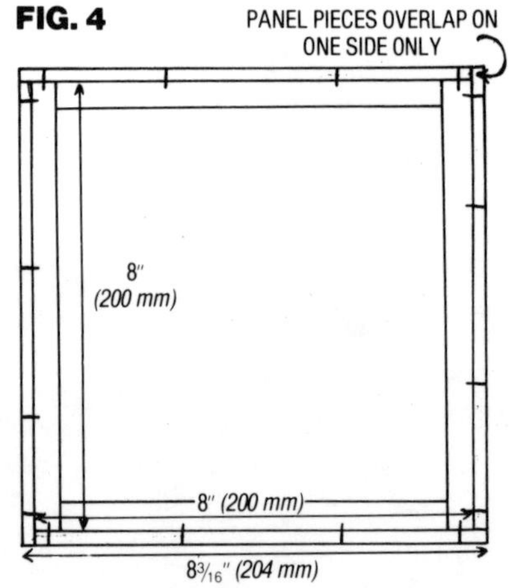

Building Instructions

Cut the plywood out as in **FIGURE 1**. You will see that some of the pieces are not square, but are longer by the thickness of the plywood. This is to make building easier. Cut the plywood to size.

Frame the square pieces (two pieces) for each cube with the molding as in **FIGURE 2**. You can miter the joints, which makes them slightly stronger, or simply butt the ends together. Glue and nail the molding flush with the outside edges on the rough or grooved side.

Glue and nail the moldings to two of the longer pieces for each cube, as in **FIGURE 3**. These will be the top and bottom pieces. Two of the longer pieces for each cube will not have any molding nailed to them until the cube is assembled.

After the glue has dried, begin assembling the cubes by holding the two square pieces vertical, and lay one of the longer pieces with the moldings on them on the top. The top piece should overlap the side pieces so that all are flush except for the one end of the top piece with the molding inset from the edge. Let that end overlap. If the top piece will not fit flush with the vertical sides, you may have to trim the ends of the inner molding on it.

Tip the cube 90°; the overlapping end of what was the top piece should be up. Glue and nail one of the pieces without a molding nailed to it so that the end is covered by the overlap and it overlaps the next piece. (See **FIGURE 4**.)

The next piece will have the moldings on it. Finish with the last piece without a molding. Be sure that all edges have been glued and nailed (there are sixteen).

Fill the voids and gaps and finish as desired.

18

Building Blocks

Toddlers love to stack and handle anything that is a manageable size for them. Penny was eighteen months old before she had the coordination to stack her blocks without them falling over at each try. By the age of two she was a master builder and could stack them as high as she wanted.

Below is a recommended list for a complete set of blocks, but do not be limited by this. Give your toddler any size he can easily manage. There should be a few of every size so that they can be matched for stacking. Cut the blocks with your miter box and saw in such a way that the ends are square. If you want to, add numbers, letters or drawings to them, using a felt-tip or any other nongreasy marker.

Penny's blocks were made from odd scraps I had left over from other projects. I gave them a cursory sanding to get rid of the splinters, rounded the corners with coarse sandpaper and applied a coat of clear sanding sealer. I sanded them lightly again after they were dry.

What You Need

LIST OF BLOCKS:

- ☐ eight 2 in. x 2 in., 3½ in. long *(38 mm x 38 mm, 89 mm long)*
- ☐ eight 2 in. x 4 in., 3½ in. long *(38 mm x 89 mm, 89 mm long)*
- ☐ eight 2 in. x 4 in., 6 in. long *(38 mm x 89 mm, 150 mm long)*
- ☐ four 1 in. x 4 in. (or plywood), 6 in. long *(17 mm x 89 mm, 150 mm long)*
- ☐ four 1 in. x 4 in. (or plywood), 10 in. long *(17 mm x 89 mm, 250 mm long)*
- ☐ four 1½ in. *(40 mm)* dowels, 3½ in. long *(89 mm)*
- ☐ four 1½ in. *(40 mm)* dowels, 6 in. long *(150 mm)*

19

Waddle Duck

This traditional toy is easy to make and delightful for the child. The duck waddles when it is pulled because the wheels are mounted off center.

Penny's duck is painted white with a red eye, an orange beak and a yellow outline for the wing. The day I completed it I had only red and yellow paint, so I mixed a bit of red with a spoonful of yellow for the proper shade of orange. The base is varnished pine.

You can use an animal or any shape for a pull toy of this type. If you have a favorite shape for a toy, cut it out, mount it on a board on wheels, and your child will enjoy trailing it along behind him.

What You Need

TOOLS: saw, hole saw, drill and bits, coping saw, saber saw or jigsaw, screwdriver

MATERIALS: 1 in. *(17 mm)* pine boards

- ☐ one piece 8 in. wide x 7 in. long *(184 mm wide x 180 mm long)*
- ☐ one piece 5½ in. wide x 7 in. long *(140 mm wide x 180 mm long)*

½ in. *(12 mm)* plywood

- ☐ one piece 6 in. *(155 mm)* square

- ☐ four 1½ in. *(40 mm)* No. 10 round-head wood screws

- ☐ two 1½ in. *(40 mm)* No. 6 flat-head wood screws

¼ in. *(6 mm)* dowels

- ☐ four ½ in. *(12 mm)*

FIG. 1

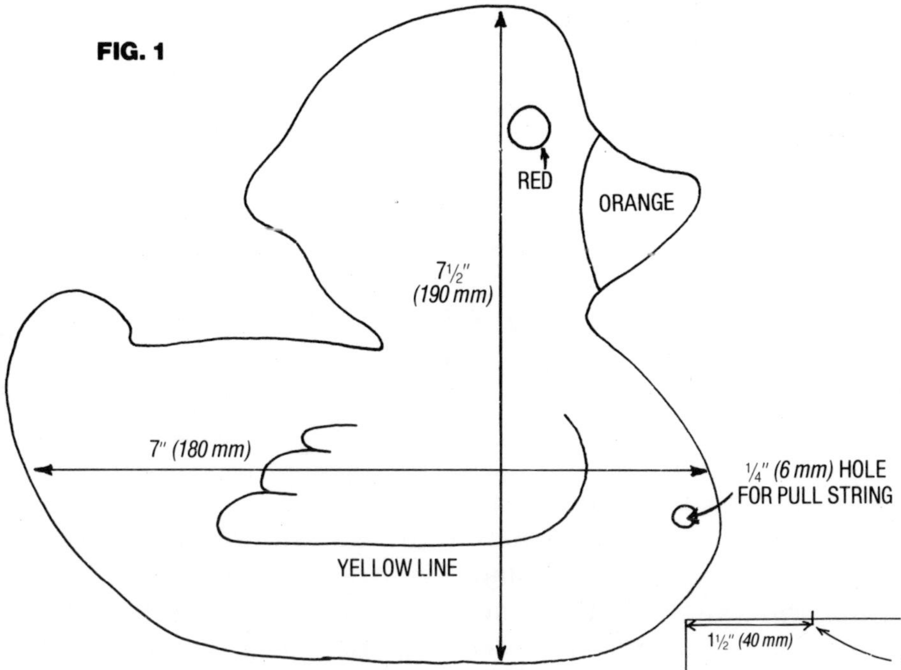

FIG. 2

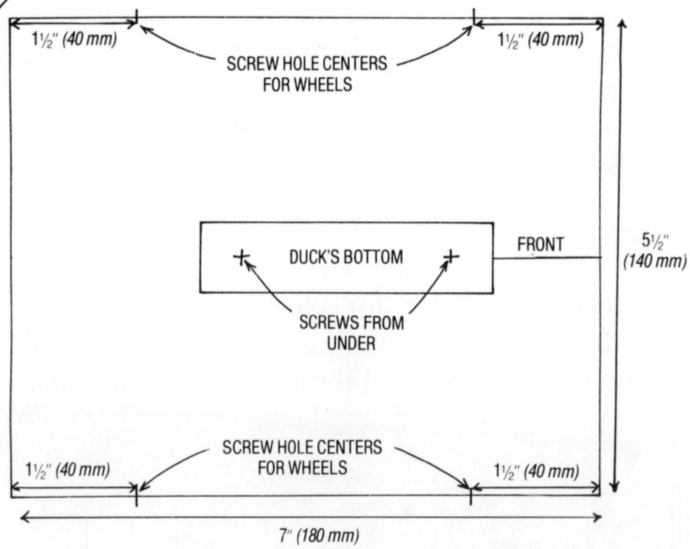

Building Instructions

I used odd scraps of pine for Penny's duck. You can use nearly any type of wood or plywood for the pieces, but plywood is best for the wheels. The base should be made from a solid board because the screws for the wheels go in from the edges.

When you draw the shape of the duck onto the wood, the grain of the wood should run along the length of the duck.

Cut the duck to shape with your coping saw, saber saw or jigsaw, and sand the edges smooth.

Mount the 2½ in. *(65 mm)* cutter in your hole saw and drill to make the four wheels from the plywood. Plug the drill hole at the center of the wheels with dowels, gluing them in place. Drill a new hole with a ¼ in. *(6 mm)* drill bit for the screw just beside the dowel after the glue has dried. This offsets the hole about ¼ in. *(6 mm)*.

Drill pilot holes for the screws in the base as shown in **FIGURE 2**, and attach the wheels. Locate the duck at the centerline of the base and drill the countersink holes and shank holes for the screws in the base as indicated. Drill a pilot hole in the duck's bottom and attach the duck.

If everything looks right, take the pieces apart and paint the duck with an undercoat, sand, and apply a coat of glossy white. After that has dried, paint on the eyes and beak. Give the base and wheels two or three coats of varnish.

Reassemble and attach a pull string about 36 in. *(900 mm)* long.

If someone accidentally steps on the duck while it is lying on its side, the head may break off. When this happened to Penny's duck, I simply dabbed the broken edges with glue and clamped the head back on. I touched up the paint, and as you can see, the toy is still in good service.

20

Rock'n'Roll

In my ongoing search for children's articles that combine several functions into one, I devised the rock 'n' roll.

One evening an older woman friend who was visiting us described an item of furniture she had enjoyed while growing up in England. Made in Scandinavia, it had been bought by her parents when on vacation there. The piece had a low seat and a curved bottom to rock on, like a rocking chair. When flipped over it became a higher seat. On its back it rolled on wheels, and when laid flat served as a low surface for coloring or drawing.

I made some preliminary sketches while our friend was there, juggled the proportions and came up with the rock 'n' roll.

The rock 'n' roll was a favorite of Penny's right from the start. I gave it to her when she was about twenty months old, and it became her first chair. She piled her Pooh Bear in it, along with other stuffed toys, and wheeled it around. She held toys on her lap as she rocked. She pushed the piece all over the house to stand on when she wanted to reach something.

As Penny got older we had to add a pad to the rocker seat to make it higher, but she still liked it for some time.

If you are making this piece for an older child, it should be both taller and deeper.

What You Need

TOOLS: saw, square, saber saw, measuring tape, hammer, clamp, drill and ½ in. *(12 mm)* and ⅝ in. *(16 mm)* bits, 2½ in. *(65 mm)* diameter hole saw for use with drill

MATERIALS:

½ in. *(12 mm)* plywood
- ☐ one piece 26 in. x 36 in. *(660 mm x 915 mm)*

½ in. *(12 mm)* dowel
- ☐ three 13 in. *(330 mm)*
- ☐ two 12 in. *(305 mm)*

¾ in. x ¾ in. *(17 mm x 17 mm)* softwood
- ☐ two 16 in. *(407 mm)*

quarter round
- ☐ two pieces 12¾ in. *(325 mm)*

☐ 1¼ in. *(32 mm)* finishing nails

☐ glue

FIG. 1

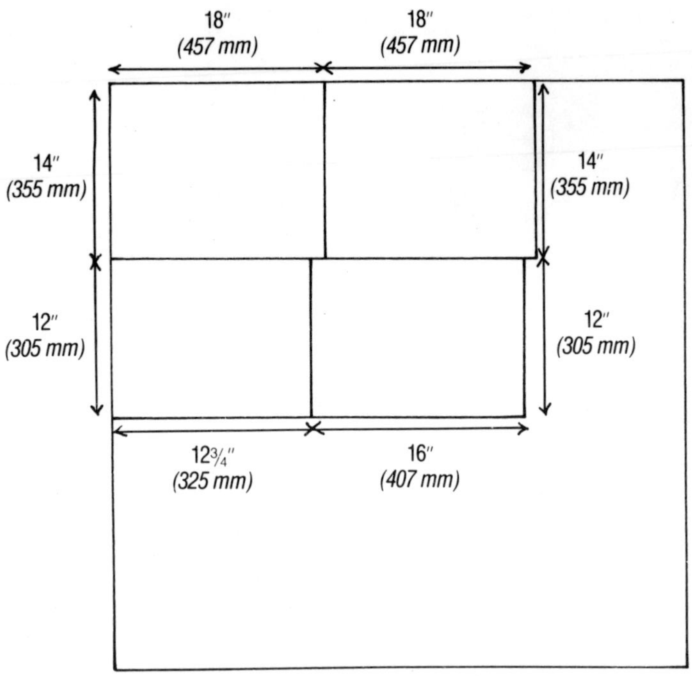

FIG. 2

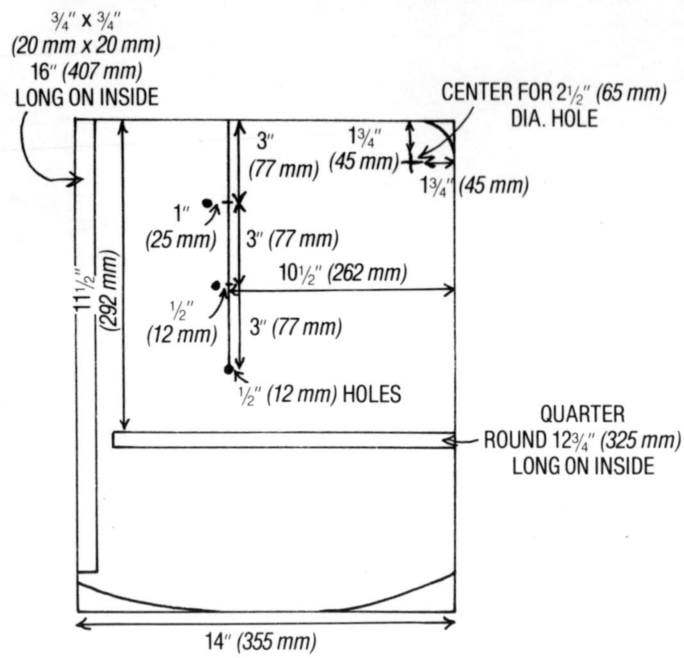

Building Instructions

Lay out the plywood pieces as in **FIGURE 1**. Before cutting the two 18 in. *(457 mm)* pieces, mark the radius for their bottom edge. The radius is 34 in. *(863 mm)* as indicated in **FIGURE 2**. I marked mine by using a yardstick (meter stick), but any piece of wood can be used. Drill a hole for a pencil tip to stick through, and a hole 34 in. *(863 mm)* from that for a nail to pivot on. The bottom of the arc should be at the midpoint of the bottom: be sure your pivoting nail is directly above this point before marking it. Do not use a string, since the string will stretch according to the degree of tension on it, and your two sides may be uneven.

Cut the curved pieces to size, using your saber saw (or coping saw) to cut the arc.

Lay out each side piece as in **FIGURE 2** to make the holes for the dowel and the 2½ in. *(65 mm)* hole for the pushing handles. Use your hole saw with the electric drill to make the 2½ in. *(65 mm)* hole, removing all but the 2½ in. *(65 mm)* cutter for the attachment from the spindle. Save these two pieces: they can be used for two of the wheels. The corner near the 2½ in. *(65 mm)* holes should be rounded on the same radius as the holes.

Cut the 16 in. *(407 mm)* pieces of ¾ in. x ¾ in. *(17 mm x 17 mm)* and drill the holes in them as in **FIGURE 3**. The ½ in. *(12 mm)* holes hold the dowels that act as axles for the wheels.

Nail and glue the ¾ in. x ¾ in. *(17 mm x 17 mm)* to the side pieces so that one end of the holes is blocked off by the sides. The ¾ in. x ¾ in. *(17 mm x 17 mm)* pieces should be on the inner side flush with the back edge of the side pieces, having the end flush with the top edge. (See **FIGURE 2**.)

Cut the holes for the wheels in the back piece as in **FIGURE 4**. The holes for the wheels do not come right to the edges because they will be glued and nailed to the inside of the ¾ in. x ¾ in. *(17 mm x 17 mm)* pieces of the side pieces. The easiest method is to drill ⅝ in. *(16 mm)* holes at the ends of the slots and then cut out the middle parts with a saber saw or coping saw.

With your hole saw make two more wheels 2½ in. *(65 mm)* in diameter. Drill the center holes out to ⅝ in. *(16 mm)* by clamping the wheels to your workshop bench or to a board or large piece of plywood. Drill only halfway through from each side to avoid splintering the plywood.

FIG. 3

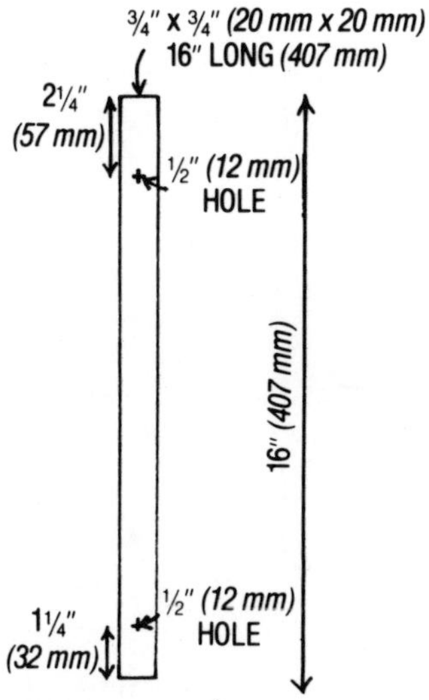

FIG. 4

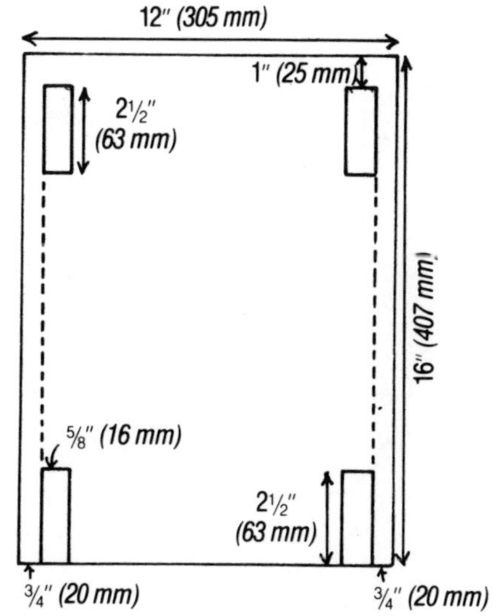

Cut the two 12 in. *(305 mm)* dowels. Round the ends slightly to remove splinters.

You are now ready to assemble the pieces. Start by sliding the wheels onto the dowels, then laying the back over the wheels so that they are properly spaced. Start the dowels in the holes in one side with the back set on the $\frac{3}{4}$ in. x $\frac{3}{4}$ in. *(17 mm x 17 mm)*. Start the other side in the same manner. When the pieces are assembled, check to make sure that the wheels turn freely and that the back is flush with the top of the side pieces. You might have to widen or lengthen the slots slightly for the wheels.

When all pieces fit well, glue and nail the back in place.

Refer again to **FIGURE 2** and you will see the $12\frac{3}{4}$ in. *(325 mm)* piece of quarter round that is the support for the seat. It will be $11\frac{1}{2}$ in. *(292 mm)* from the top edge of the sides, with one end nailed and glued to each side on the inside surface. The seat should slide easily in place on top of it and can be nailed and glued.

Cut the three 13 in. *(330 mm)* dowels and fit them into the holes on the sides. Dab glue on the holes and near the ends of the dowels, and then tap the dowels with your hammer until they are flush. I put a nail or two in the ends to make the ends tight in the holes.

Use your wood filler and sandpaper, and finish as desired.

21

Indoor Gym

At the age of eighteen to twenty months a child needs a lot of exercise to flex his newfound leg, back and arm muscles. He also needs to try out his balance and stretch his body to the limit. He enjoys having a place of his own to crawl into.

The small indoor gym is designed for a child of this age group. By the time he is four years old he will likely become bored by the shortness of the slide and the lack of thrills, but for a couple of years the gym is sure to be a well-used plaything.

Parents will appreciate this piece because of its easy construction. There are no complicated joints, and everything goes together with glue and nails. If you wish to be able to dismantle it, use screws to fasten the top and end pieces and the ladder rungs.

Using common ½ in. *(12 mm)* plywood and pine, you can build the gym inexpensively and complete the construction, excluding painting, in roughly four hours. It is possible to cut the pieces for both the gym and the toy box from the same sheet of plywood with very little waste. If you use "good one side" plywood, you will have to fill a couple of voids. You can get "good both sides" plywood for a few dollars more.

What You Need

TOOLS: saw, square, drill and bits, measuring tape, saber saw. Optional: miter box and saw, Surform file or rasp

MATERIALS:

2 in. x 2 in. *(38 mm x 38 mm)* pine or fir, common grade
- ☐ four pieces 40 in. *(1015 mm)*
- ☐ four pieces 36 in. *(915 mm)*

1 in. *(25 mm)* softwood or hardwood dowels
- ☐ three 17 in. *(431 mm)*
- ☐ two 22 in. *(558 mm)*
- ☐ one 15½ in. *(394 mm)*

1 in. x 2 in. *(17 mm x 38 mm)* pine or fir
- ☐ two pieces 20¼ in. *(515 mm)*
- ☐ one piece 11 in. *(280 mm)*
- ☐ one piece 50 in. *(1270 mm)*

Do not cut the last two pieces to the exact length, since they will be cut on an angle later to make two pieces each.

¼ in. *(6 mm)* plywood

- ☐ one piece 13½ in. x 33⅝ in. *(342 mm x 855 mm)*
- ☐ glue
- ☐ 1¼ in. *(32 mm)* finishing nails
- ☐ twelve 2½ in. *(65 mm)* nails
- ☐ one sheet ½ in. *(12 mm)* plywood, "good one side" or better grade to suit.

FIG. 1

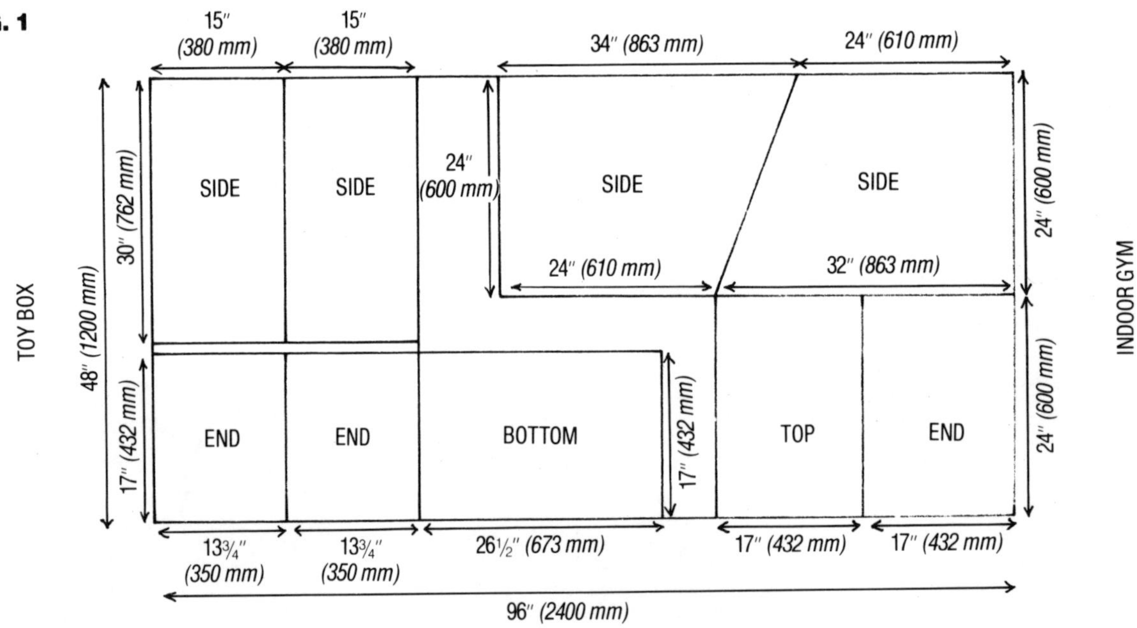

Building Instructions

Lay out the plywood for the gym and the toy box as in **FIGURE 1.** Cut out these pieces and smooth the rough saw-cut edges with sandpaper.

Cut the 2 in. x 2 in. *(38 mm x 38 mm)* and the 20¼ in. *(515 mm)* 1 in. x 2 in. *(17 mm x 38 mm)* and the 1 in. *(25 mm)* dowels to length. Drill the holes for the handrails in the 2 in. x 2 in. *(38 mm x 38 mm)* as in **FIGURE 2.** Insert the handrails into the holes before gluing and nailing the 2 in. x 2 in. *(38 mm x 38 mm)* to the side pieces. The 2 in. x 2 in. *(38 mm x 38 mm)* at the square end should be inset from the edge the thickness of the plywood, and the other parallel to it but 24 in. *(610 mm)* from that same edge to the outside edge of the 2 in. x 2 in. *(38 mm x 38 mm).* When you lay these pieces out, before fastening the 2 in. x 2 in. *(38 mm x 38 mm)*, be sure you have them marked so that when the side pieces are upright and parallel with the slanted ends pointed in the same direction, the 2 in. x 2 in. *(38 mm x 38 mm)* will be on the inside.

Nail and glue the 20¼ in. *(515 mm)* pieces of 1 in. x 2 in. *(17 mm x 38 mm)* between the 2 in. x 2 in. *(38 mm x 38 mm)* at each side, with the upper edge 3 in. *(77 mm)* below the upper edge of the plywood.

To cut the 1 in. x 2 in. *(17 mm x 38 mm)* pieces that hold the ladder rungs, begin by laying one side piece on the plywood side. Lay a 2 in. x 2 in. *(38 mm x 38 mm)* piece along the slanted edge, then lay a 1

FIG. 2

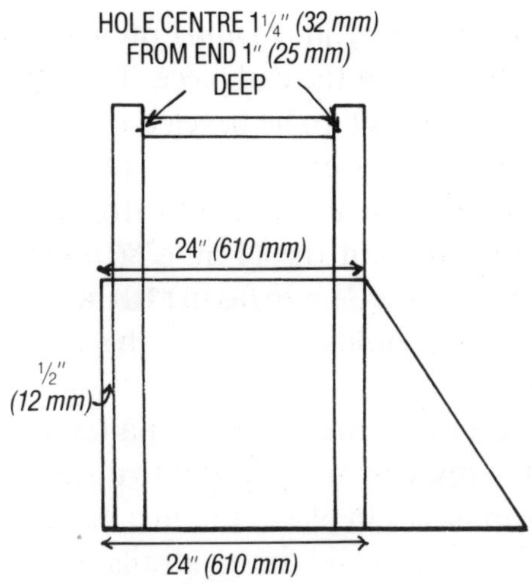

FIG. 3

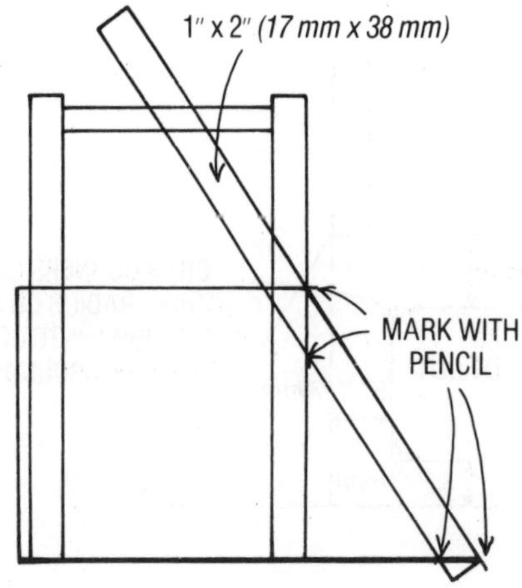

FIG. 3A

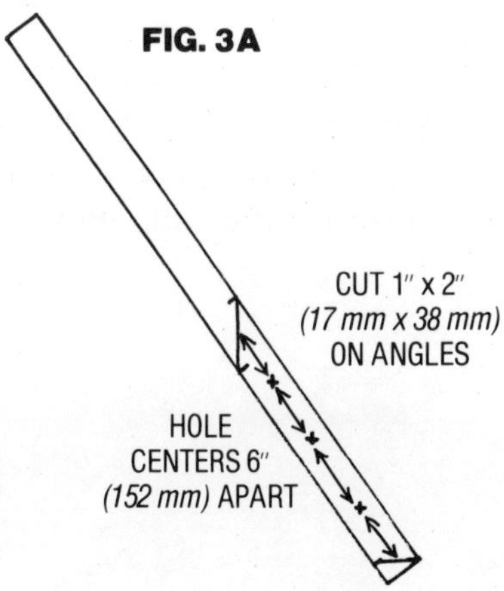

FIG. 4

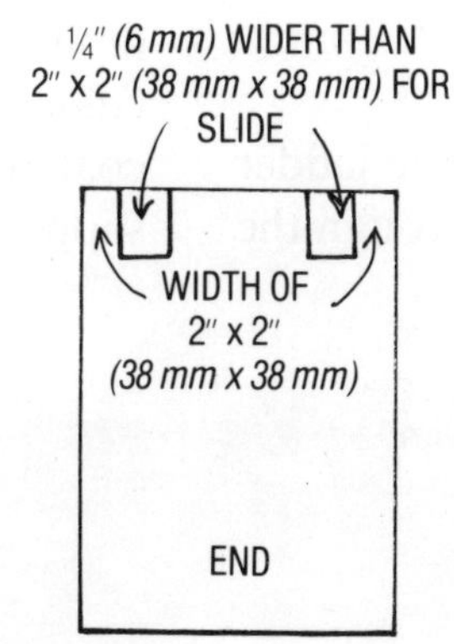

FIG. 5

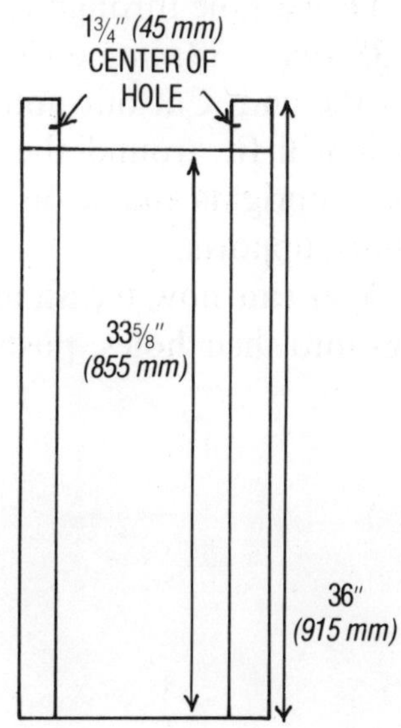

FIG. 6

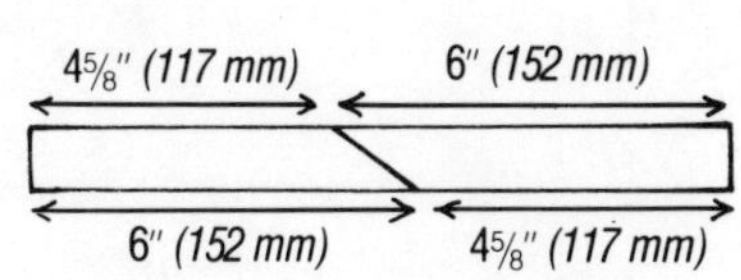

in. x 2 in. *(17 mm x 38 mm)* on top of that piece. This will allow you to mark the angle cuts accurately at both ends by marking the sides where the cuts will end, and making the cut after the board is moved. If you make the long-angled cut accurately on the first side, you will not have to mark it for the other side, since it will already be cut at the proper angle. (See **FIGURE 3**.)

Drill the holes for the rungs as in **FIGURE 3**. Nail and glue the 1 in. x 2 in. *(17 mm x 38 mm)* pieces in place.

Cut two notches in the end piece as in **FIGURE 4**.

Drill the holes for the dowel that holds the slide $16\frac{1}{4}$ in. *(413 mm)* down from the top of the end-corner 2 in. x 2 in. *(38 mm x 38 mm)* pieces on their inside edges using your 1 in. *(25 mm)* drill. These holes should be about $\frac{3}{4}$ in. *(20 mm)* deep.

Make the slide by gluing and nailing the $\frac{1}{4}$ in. *(6 mm)* plywood to the two 36 in. *(915 mm)* pieces of 2 in. x 2 in. *(38 mm x 38 mm)* as in **FIGURE 5**. These pieces should be flush with the edges of the plywood on three edges, the bottom ends and both sides. Glue and nail the other two 36 in. *(915 mm)* pieces of 2 in. x 2 in. *(38 mm x 38 mm)* directly on top of the former two, sandwiching the plywood between them. Use the $2\frac{1}{2}$ in. *(65 mm)* nails to fasten them together, nailing some in from both sides.

FIG.7

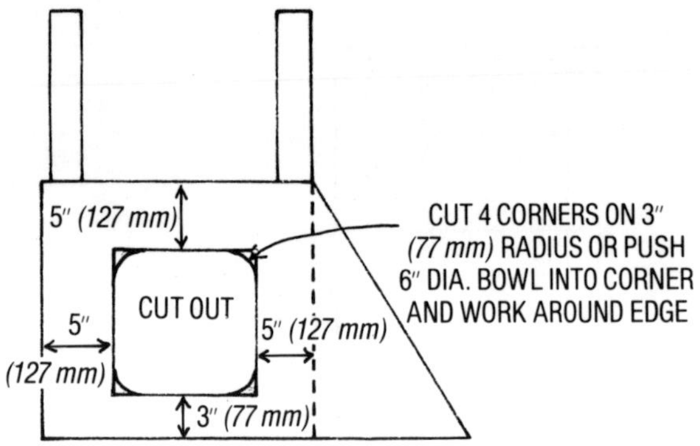

Drill a hole through each of the lower 2 in. x 2 in. *(38 mm x 38 mm)* on the slide 1¾ in. *(45 mm)* from the end. Cut out notches in the top piece so that it will fit around the 2 in. x 2 in. *(38 mm x 38 mm)* uprights and lie on the 1 in. x 2 in. *(17 mm x 38 mm)* supports.

You can now try an assembly. Fit the ladder rungs into their holes, push the dowel through the slide and start the dowel ends in their respective holes. Put the end piece in place and see if the whole piece is square.

The edge of the ¼ in. *(6 mm)* plywood slide should lie on the edge of the end piece. The top edge of the end piece will need to be beveled off, to allow the slide to sit properly on the floor. Disassemble the piece and bevel with a rasp or a Surform file.

Reassemble and cut the 11 in. *(280 mm)* piece of 1 in. x 2 in. *(17 mm x 38 mm)* as in **FIGURE 6**. Glue and nail it so that it holds the end of the slide 3 in. *(77 mm)* off the floor.

When everything fits properly, nail and glue, or fasten with screws if you wish later to disassemble the end and top pieces in place. Put in a nail at each end of the ladder rungs and the handrails, as well, to keep them from turning in their holes.

Lay out the holes in the sides as in **FIGURE 7**, and cut out, using your saber saw, after drilling a starter hole.

Round and sand the edges and corners as desired, then finish with paint or varnish. Bright colors of paint are especially pleasing, and several coats of urethane varnish on the slide will make it slippery.

22

Table & Stool

Children love having furniture scaled down to their size, and a table for a child's first efforts at drawing will be greatly appreciated. I hit upon the following design when trying to devise a simple method of constructing a small table with legs of adjustable lengths as well as a shelf for storage.

The table is proportioned to suit a child of two years. The tabletop could be increased in size for a larger child, perhaps 20 in. x 24 in. or 28 in. *(510 mm x 610 mm or 710 mm)* with legs 20 in. to 22 in. *(510 mm to 560 mm)* high. **FIGURE 4** shows how to make the legs adjustable for raising the table height as the child grows.

The stool is reminiscent of the old-time milkmaid's stool used on dairy farms. A three-legged stool does not wobble if set on an uneven surface, nor if the legs are not exactly the same length. The construction, therefore, is foolproof.

What You Need

TOOLS: saw, square, tape measure, hammer, drill and adjustable bit

MATERIALS:

½ in. *(12 mm)* plywood
- ☐ one piece 26 in. x 48 in. *(660 mm x 1220 mm)*

2 in. x 3 in. *(38 mm x 64 mm)* pine, fir or spruce
- ☐ two pieces 16 in. *(407 mm)*

1 in. *(25 mm)* hardwood dowels
- ☐ three 7½ in. *(190 mm)*

- ☐ 1½ in. *(38 mm)* finishing nails
- ☐ 1 in. *(25 mm)* finishing nails
- ☐ glue

Jeans
Jeans
Jeans
Jeans
Jeans

FIG. 1

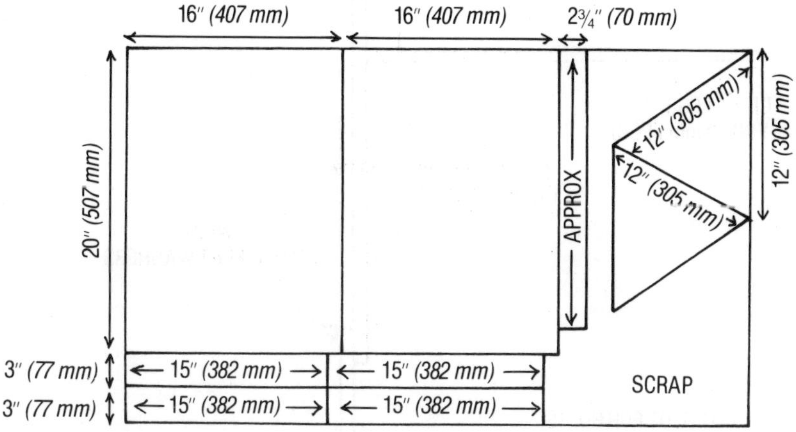

FIG. 3

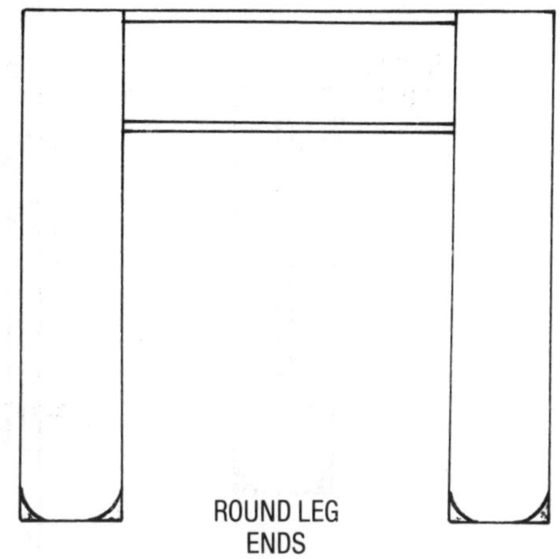

FIG. 2

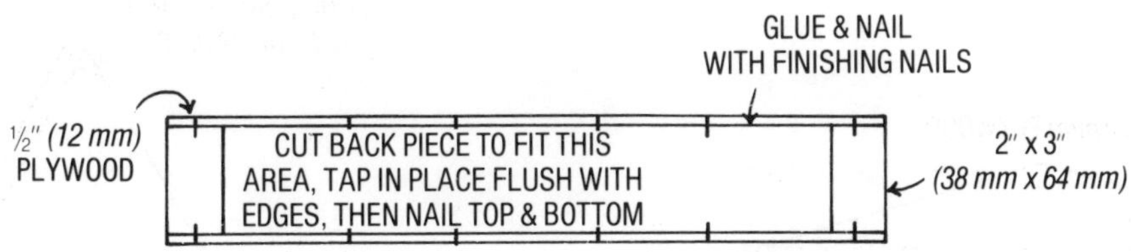

Building Instructions

Mark out the pieces of plywood as in **FIGURE 1**, cutting out all except the back piece. Do not cut this piece until the table is partially assembled, since the size may vary.

The two largest pieces are the top and shelf. I painted the underside of the top and the top side of the shelf as well as one side of the 2 in. x 3 in. *(38 mm x 64 mm)* pieces before constructing the table, since it would be difficult to paint these inside areas on an assembled table. If you do paint before assembling, leave a strip 1½ in. *(38 mm)* wide unpainted along the side that is 16 in. *(407 mm)* long where the 2 in. x 3 in. *(38 mm x 64 mm)* piece will be glued and nailed. The glue will not stick properly to a painted surface.

Begin assembling the table by placing the 2 in. x 3 in. *(38 mm x 64 mm)* on edge and smearing the edges with glue. Then place one of the 16 in. x 20 in. *(407 mm x 507 mm)* pieces on top of it, with the ends and edges of the 2 in. x 3 in. *(38 mm x 64 mm)* flush with the ends and edges of the plywood. If you are using "good one side" plywood, be sure that the good side of the top and shelf will be facing up. Nail the pieces in place with the 1½ in. *(38 mm)* finishing nails.

Turn the pieces over and similarly nail the other piece of plywood in place. The project should now resemble **FIGURE 2**.

Cut the back piece to fit between the 2 in. x 3 in. *(38 mm x 64 mm)* and the upper and lower pieces of plywood, flush with the back. Cut it as close to the exact size as possible; this is an important structural piece, and a tight fit helps prevent the table from working loose and wobbling. Nail in place with nails going in from the top and bottom.

At this point I rounded the corners of the bottom of the legs and gave them a cursory sanding. Attach the legs as in **FIGURE 3**, using glue and nails.

If your table is larger or higher than the above and may have several children vying for space around it, you could use ¾ in. *(18 mm)* plywood for the legs and attach them with 2 in. *(50 mm)* No. 8 round-head wood screws.

You can glue and nail three of the legs onto the table, having the tops of the legs flush with the top of the table, without worrying about the table wobbling. It is the fourth leg that is critical. Put the table on a surface that you know is flat, such as a tabletop, and set the leg in place. If it must project above the surface of the tabletop to keep the other

22-Fig 4

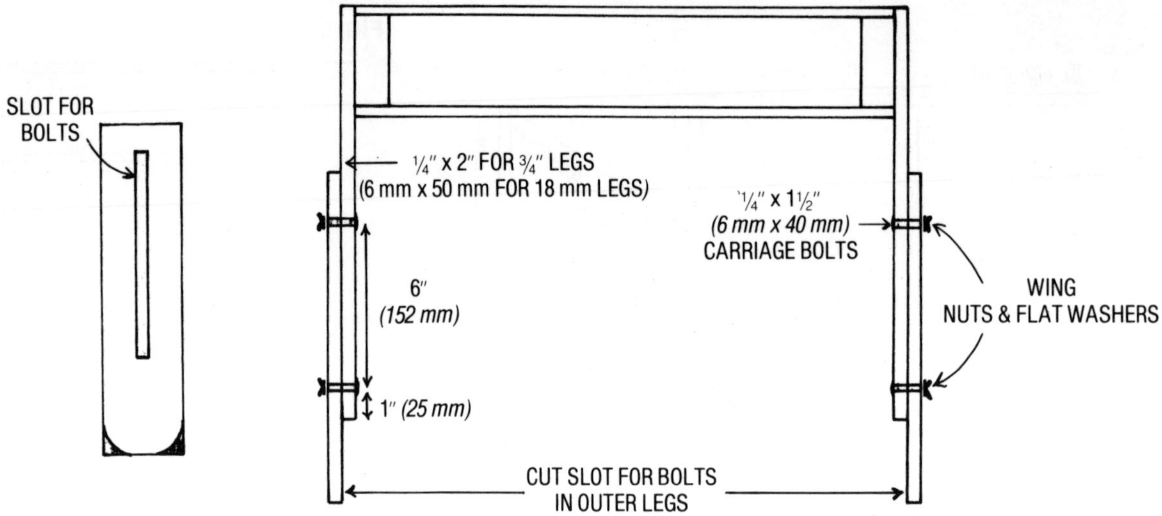

22—Fig 6

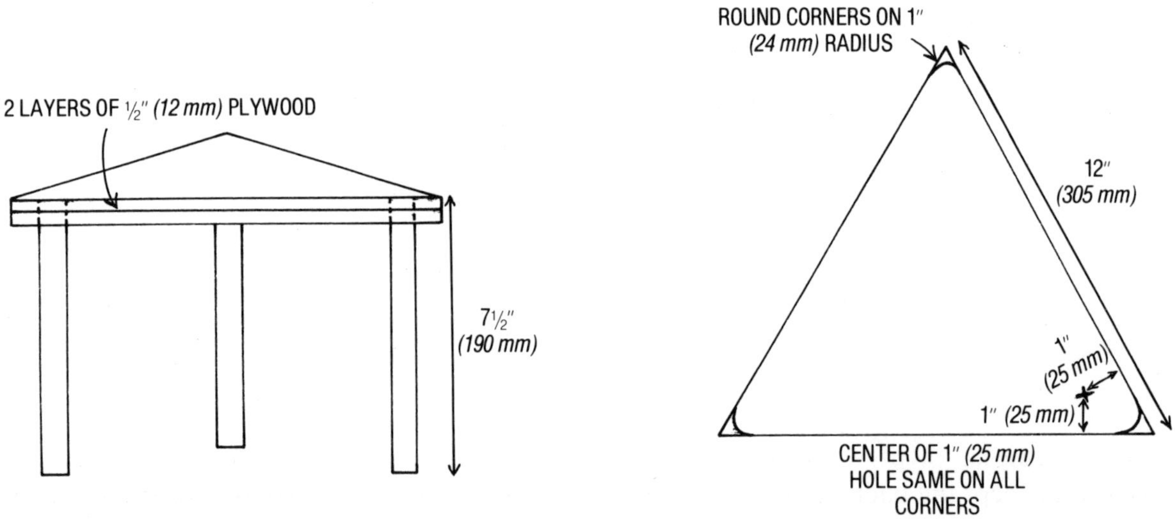

legs from wobbling, cut a bit off. If it must be below the top surface, just glue and nail it in place, since the difference should be slight.

If you would like to make the table with an adjustable height, or wish to add extensions for the legs as the child grows, refer to **FIGURE 4**. The extension would be the width of the legs, and the slot should not come closer than 2 in. *(50 mm)* from the ends. The slot should be just wide enough for the bolts to slide easily. The bolts should be at least 6 in. *(152 mm)* apart. Using the above formula, a 12 in. *(305 mm)* extension would raise the table a maximum of 3 in. *(77 mm).*

To construct the stool, cut out the two triangles of plywood and glue and nail them together, one on top of the other, with the 1 in. *(25 mm)* nails. Do not put any nails near the corners where the 1 in. *(25 mm)* holes will be drilled. Mark each corner as in the lower right corner of the triangle in **FIGURE 5**. Make a mark parallel to the sides 1 in. *(25 mm)* from the edge. Where the two lines cross, drill a hole the size of the dowel.

I specify an adjustable bit because dowels are often not exactly the dimension specified. Experiment with a few trial holes until the adjustable bit is set to give a hole in which the dowel will fit tightly. The dowel must be held tightly since there is nothing else to keep the legs of the stool rigid.

Drill the holes from one side until the point breaks through, then turn the plywood piece over and complete the hole. This gives a much neater hole. When the holes are drilled, round off the corners to a 1 in. *(25 mm)* radius or any other pleasing shape.

Cut the dowel legs 7½ in. *(190 mm)* long, smear some glue around the holes in the double layer of plywood and insert the dowels. Tap them in until they are flush with the top surface. Then set a nail from the two nearby edges into the dowel to hold it in place.

Begin the finishing by using your wood filler around the back piece and legs of the table and the legs of the stool. Fill the voids in the edges of the plywood and sand and paint as desired.

23

Single Bed

When Penny was ready to move out of her crib into her own single bed, time and space were at a premium. We wanted to get her settled before her baby brother arrived, and since the children were to share a room, the bed had to be economical in size.

Bunk beds were out of the question, but what I designed was like the lower part of the bunk beds, with rails around one level and a mattress only 5 ft. *(1520 mm)* long. I used construction-grade pine and varnished it. The bed looked very nice, and Penny could not fall out with her restless tossing so typical of toddlers. Many friends with similar space problems commented favorably—and Penny loved her new quarters.

The mattress is 30 in. *(760 mm)* wide, sufficient for a small child. The length is adequate for an average child up until his middle years, when he gets his growth spurt. The bed could, of course, be made longer by adding another 12 in. *(305 mm)* to the side pieces.

Beds of this type were often made by the early North American settlers. You can see them in any pioneer village you might visit.

What You Need

TOOLS: saw, square, drill and bits, screwdriver, wrench, hammer, miter box and saw, spokeshave or Surform file

MATERIALS:

2 in. x 4 in. *(38 mm x 89 mm)* pine
- ☐ two pieces 63 in. *(1600 mm)*
- ☐ two pieces 30 in. *(762 mm)*

2 in. x 2 in. *(38 mm x 38 mm)* pine
- ☐ four pieces 25½ in. *(648 mm)*

¾ in. *(18 mm)* softwood dowels
- ☐ twenty-nine 10 in. *(254 mm)*

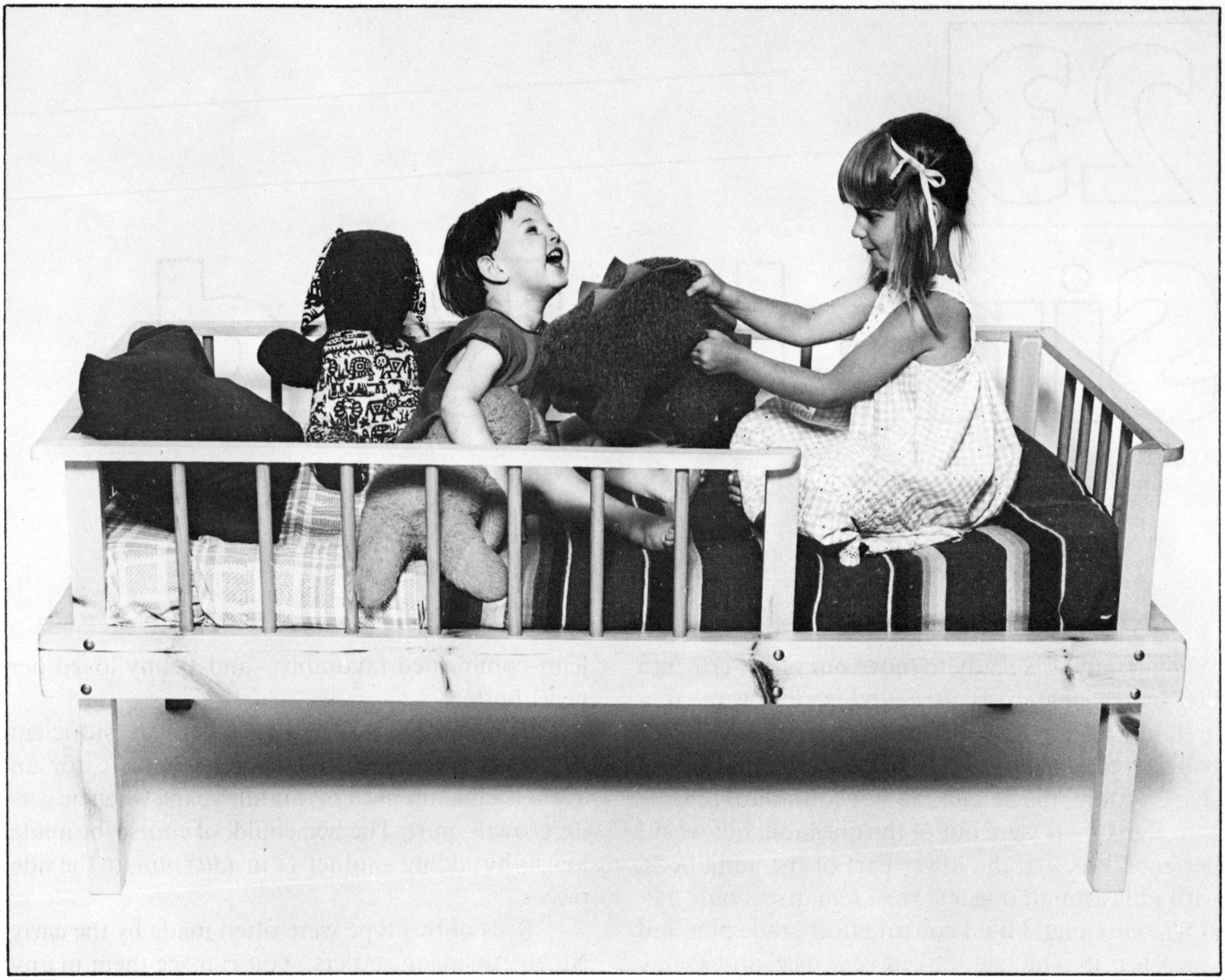

1 in. x 2 in. *(17 mm x 38 mm)* spruce (can be rough)
- ☐ two pieces 57 in. *(1445 mm)*
- ☐ two pieces 27 in. *(680 mm)*

1 in. x 2 in. *(17 mm x 38 mm)* clear pine
- ☐ one piece 63 in. *(1600 mm)*
- ☐ one piece 33 in. *(838 mm)*
- ☐ one piece 31½ in. *(800 mm)*
- ☐ one piece 41 in. *(1041 mm)*
- ☐ one piece 13½ in. *(343 mm)*

carriage bolts with flat washers
- ☐ eight ¼ in. x 3 in. *(6 mm x 75 mm)*
- ☐ two ¼ in. x 2½ in. *(6 mm x 120 mm)*

☐ fourteen 1½ in. *(40 mm)* No. 8 flat-head wood screws

☐ 1 in. *(25 mm)* finishing nails

☐ ½ in. *(12 mm)* chipboard for mattress support
one piece 29¾ in. x 59¾ in. *(755 mm x 1832 mm)*

☐ 4 in. *(100 mm)* foam mattress, 30 in. x 60 in. *(760 mm x 1520 mm)* with cloth to cover. A 6 ft. *(1800 mm)* foam slab is easily cut to length with a serrated knife.

Building Instructions

Begin by cutting the 2 in. x 4 in. *(38 mm x 89 mm)* and the 2 in. x 2 in. *(38 mm x 38 mm)* pine to length. The 2 in. x 2 in. *(38 mm x 38 mm)* pieces are the legs, so bolt the 30 in. *(762 mm)* 2 in. x 4 in. *(38 mm x 89 mm)* pieces 12 in. *(305 mm)* up from one end. The ends should be flush with the legs. Use two bolts per end, and countersink the nut and washer. The countersink hole should be ¾ in. *(20 mm)* in diameter and on the inside—that is, on the leg, not the 2 in. x 4 in. *(38 mm x 89 mm)*.

The 63 in. *(1600 mm)* pieces of 2 in. x 4 in. *(38 mm x 89 mm)* can then be bolted on, their ends flush with the outside edges of the 30 in. *(762 mm)* pieces. Your frame should resemble **FIGURE 1** from the top view.

Using the two remaining carriage bolts, attach the 13½ in. *(343 mm)* piece of clear pine 1 in. x 2 in. *(17 mm x 38 mm)*, as shown in **FIGURE 1**, with its lower end flush with the bottom of the 2 in. x 4 in. *(38 mm x 89 mm)*. Be sure it is square with the side pieces and that its top is not higher than the top ends of the legs.

Cut the 1 in. x 2 in. *(17 mm x 38 mm)* clear pine to length, and miter the ends for three corners. The pieces by the opening (see **FIGURE 2**) will have the corners rounded.

Mark out the holes for the dowels on the 2 in. x 4 in. *(38 mm x 89 mm)* on its top side. The dowel centers are 4½ in. *(115 mm)* apart. (See **FIGURE 3**.) There will be five dowels on the ends, seven dowels on the front and twelve dowels at the back. The 4½ in. *(115 mm)* spaces should be measured from the corners of the legs, not the corners of the frame. The spaces will work out exactly for the front, not quite so exactly for the ends, but the back will have a smaller gap between the last dowel and the leg.

Hold or clamp the 1 in. x 2 in. *(17 mm x 38 mm)* beside the 2 in. x 4 in. *(38 mm x 89 mm)* over which it will later be fixed, and mark the holes for the dowels on both pieces at the same time. Note that the holes for the dowels will be drilled on the underside of the 1 in. x 2 in. *(17 mm x 38 mm)*: it should be turned over for marking.

FIG. 1

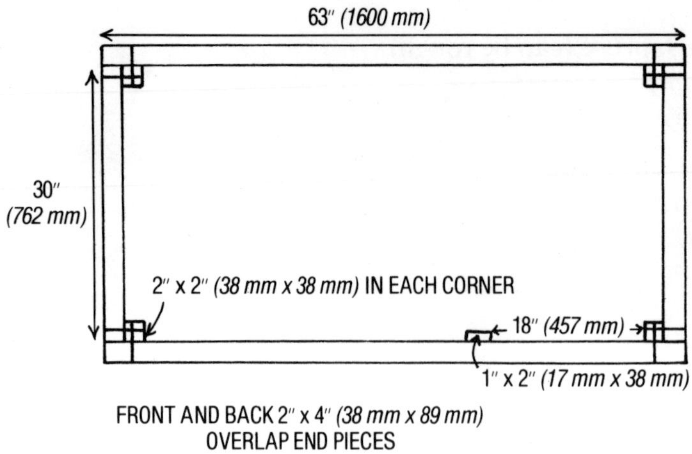

FIG. 3

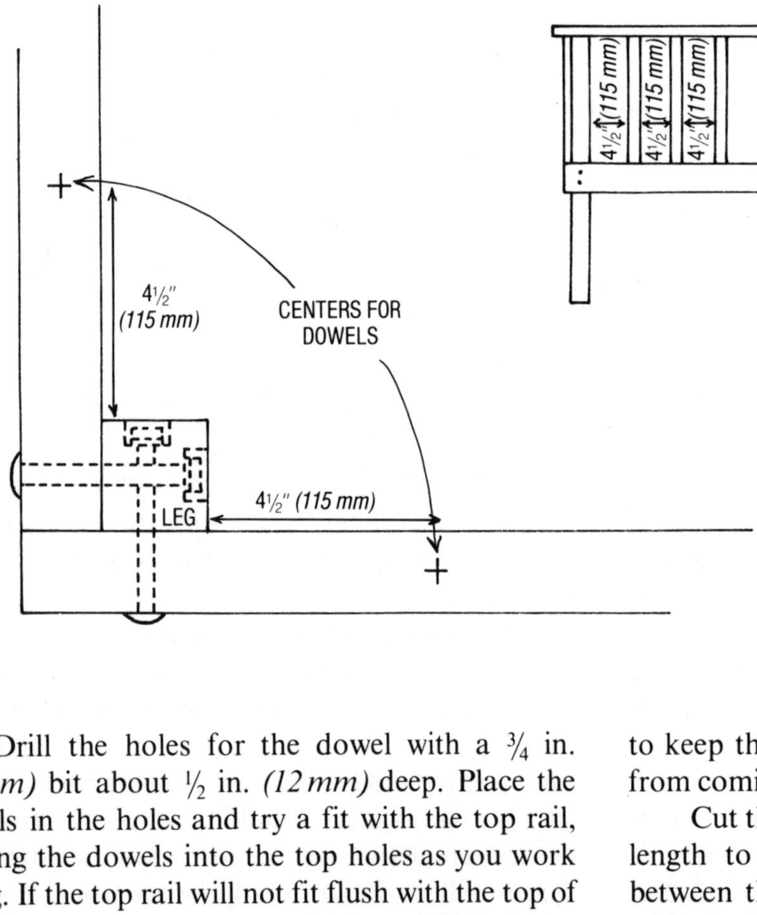

FIG. 2

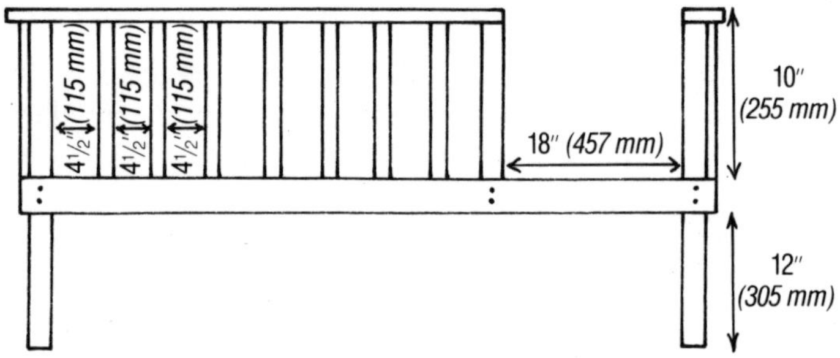

Drill the holes for the dowel with a ¾ in. *(18 mm)* bit about ½ in. *(12 mm)* deep. Place the dowels in the holes and try a fit with the top rail, moving the dowels into the top holes as you work along. If the top rail will not fit flush with the top of the leg corner posts, you may have to drill the holes deeper.

When everything fits well, drill a ⅜ in. *(10 mm)* hole about two-thirds of the way through the 1 in. x 2 in. *(17 mm x 38 mm)* from the outside edge, and set a screw through this hole into the corner post.

Set a nail into the top and bottom of each dowel. Nail from the outside edge of the top and bottom rails. The nails should angle into the dowels to keep them from turning, and also to keep them from coming out if the top rail is lifted.

Cut the 1 in. x 2 in. *(17 mm x 38 mm)* spruce to length to fit on the inside of the frame, going between the legs. Its bottom edge should be flush with the bottom edge of the side and end frame pieces. Fix them in place with the remaining screws.

Cut the piece of chipboard to fit, cutting out the corners for the legs and a slot for the 1 in. x 2 in. *(17 mm x 38 mm)* at the opening. Round the inner corners of the legs with a spokeshave or Surform file.

I gave Penny's bed four coats of urethane varnish.

24

Bunk Beds

At the age of two to three years a child is ready to sleep in a regular bed. The bunk bed illustrated has side and end rails with uprights to keep him from rolling out. It has room for a friend, and when draped over with a spare sheet it can become the child's personal space.

If constructed as directed the bunk beds can be dismantled, with the ends coming off and the side pieces remaining whole. Use a 6 in. *(150 mm)* foam mattress or a regular mattress. The design is for a mattress 36 in. *(915 mm)* wide, but for a wider or narrower mattress just change the length of all the pieces along the ends.

The bunk beds are best varnished since a natural finish enhances their rustic appearance.

What You Need

TOOLS: saw, square, tape measure, drill and bits, hammer, socket wrench

MATERIALS:

2 in. x 6 in. *(38 mm x 140 mm)* pine, fir or cedar
- ☐ four pieces 72 in. *(1830 mm)*
- ☐ four pieces 42½ in. *(1080 mm)*

2 in. x 4 in. *(38 mm x 89 mm)* pine, fir or cedar
- ☐ five pieces 64 in. *(1625 mm)*

2 in. x 2 in. *(38 mm x 38 mm)* pine, fir or cedar
- ☐ four pieces 42½ in. *(1080 mm)*
- ☐ one piece 56½ in. *(1435 mm)*
- ☐ one piece 35 in. *(889 mm)*
- ☐ one piece 16 in. *(405 mm)*

1 in. x 2 in. *(17 mm x 38 mm)* pine, fir or cedar
- ☐ two pieces 72 in. *(1830 mm)*
- ☐ two pieces 34½ in. *(877 mm)*

1 in. *(25 mm)* hardwood dowels
- ☐ six pieces 14 in. *(355 mm)*

¾ in. *(18 mm)* softwood dowels
- ☐ thirty-nine 10 in. *(254 mm)*

½ in. *(12 mm)* particle board or chipboard
☐ two pieces 4 ft. x 8 ft. *(1200 mm x 2400 mm)*

☐ twenty-four ¼ in. x 4 in. *(6 mm x 100 mm)* lag bolts and flat washers

carriage bolts and flat washers
☐ eleven ¼ in. x 4 in. *(6 mm x 100 mm)*
☐ fifteen ¼ in. x 3 in. *(6 mm x 75 mm)*

☐ thirty-six 1½ in. *(40 mm)* No. 8 flat-head wood screws

☐ 1 in. *(25 mm)* finishing nails

FIG. 1

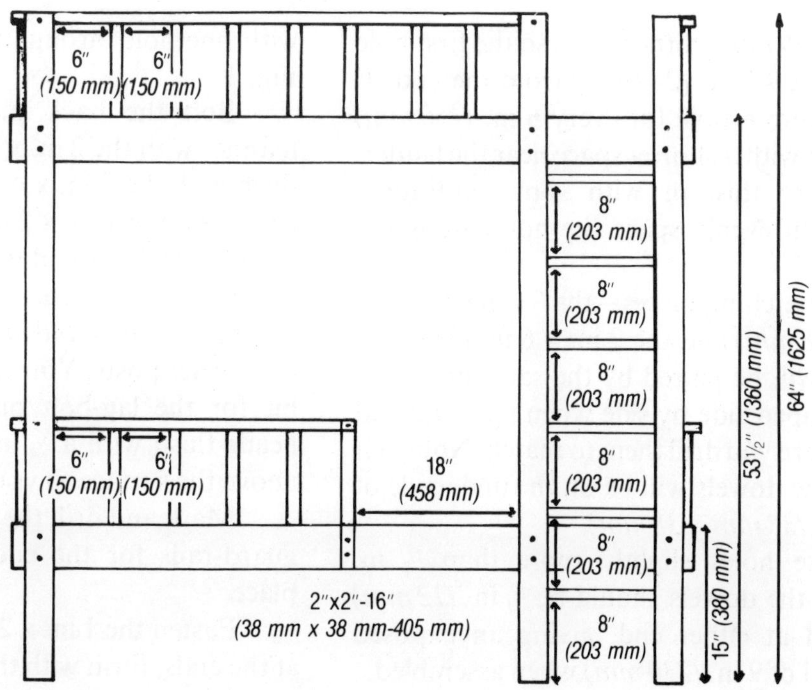

Building Instructions

The completed bunk beds should look as in **FIGURE 1**. The 2 in. x 4 in. *(38 mm x 89 mm)* pieces form the corner posts and the second upright for the ladder; the 2 in. x 6 in. *(38 mm x 140 mm)* pieces form the frames for the mattresses. The 1 in. x 2 in. *(17 mm x 38 mm)* pieces are bolted inside the 2 in. x 6 in. *(38 mm x 140 mm)* pieces as supports for the particle board or chipboard. The 2 in. x 2 in. *(38 mm x 38 mm)* pieces are the guardrails and the ¾ in. *(18 mm)* dowels go from the 2 in. x 2 in. *(38 mm x 38 mm)* to the 2 in. x 6 in. *(38 mm x 140 mm)*. The 1 in. *(25 mm)* dowels are for the ladder rungs.

The beds have no guardrails at the back, since they are intended to be set against a wall. If necessary, a rail with dowels could be added, using the same dimensions of stock as for the other rails and dowels.

Begin by cutting to size all of the pieces that form the front of the bunk beds as in **FIGURE 1**. Drill the holes for the 1 in. *(25 mm)* dowels (for the ladder rungs) on the edges of the 2 in. x 4 in. *(38 mm x 89 mm)*. They should be 1 in. *(25 mm)* deep so that when assembled the 2 in. x 4 in. *(38 mm x 89 mm)* will be 12 in. *(305 mm)* apart. The holes for the dowels are centered 10 in. *(254 mm)* apart, and there are five rungs.

The holes for the ¾ in. *(18 mm)* dowels will be along the edges of the 2 in. x 2 in. *(38 mm x 38 mm)* and the 2 in. x 6 in. *(38 mm x 140 mm)*. These dowels should be on 6 in. *(150 mm)* centers as in **FIGURE 2**. If measuring from the head of the bed, remember that these pieces will go behind the 2 in. x

FIG. 2

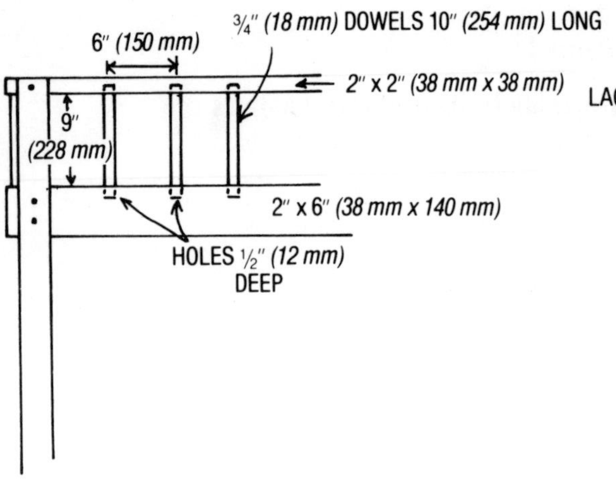

FIG. 3

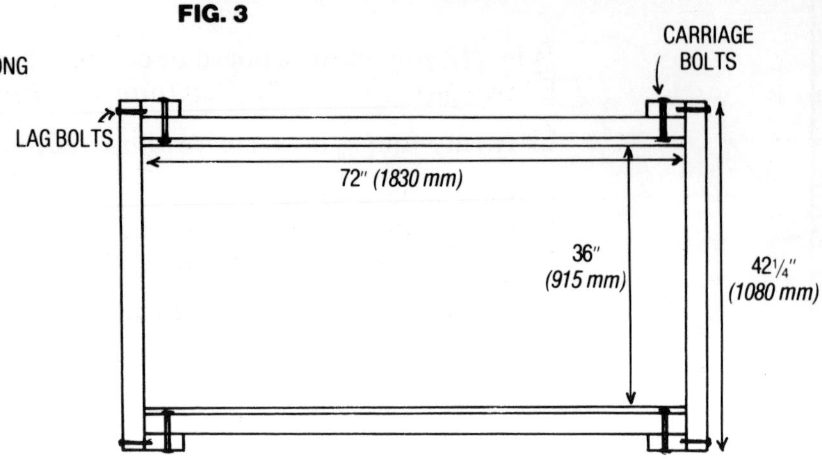

4 in. *(38 mm x 89 mm)* corner post, so the first hole should be about 9½ in. *(240 mm)* from the end. If you then measure a hole for every 6 in. *(150 mm)* you will end up with a shorter space near the ladder. You can ignore this, or with some additional figuring you can evenly space the holes along the rail.

The two matching pieces—that is the 2 in. x 2 in. *(38 mm x 38 mm)* and the 2 in. x 6 in. *(38 mm x 140 mm)* that will be paired by the same dowels—should be clamped side by side when marking and drilling to be sure you drill them to match. Note that the holes for the dowels will be on the underside of the 2 in. x 2 in. *(38 mm x 38 mm)*.

Drill these holes slightly more than ½ in. *(12 mm)* deep; the dowels should be ½ in. *(12 mm)* into the wood at either end, giving an exposed length of dowel of 9 in. *(230 mm)* when assembled.

Begin assembling the front frame by bolting the 2 in. x 6 in. *(38 mm x 140 mm)* pieces to the 2 in. x 4 in. *(38 mm x 89 mm)* corner posts, with the heads of the bolts countersunk about ¼ in. *(6 mm)* on the outside, and the washer and nut end countersunk on the inside as in **FIGURE 1**. Attach the 72 in. *(1830 mm)* of the 1 in. x 2 in. *(17 mm x 38 mm)* along the bottom edge of each 2 in. x 6 in. *(38 mm x 140 mm)* so that the lower bolt goes through the corner post, the 2 in. x 6 in. *(38 mm x 140 mm)* and the 1 in. x 2 in. *(17 mm x 38 mm)*. The lower carriage bolt is 4 in. *(100 mm)* long: the upper bolt is 3 in. *(75 mm)* long.

Assemble the ladder by inserting the 1 in. *(25 mm)* dowels into their holes, and bolt on the other 2 in. x 4 in. *(38 mm x 89 mm)* ladder side.

The 16 in. *(405 mm)* piece of 2 in. x 2 in. *(38 mm x 38 mm)* supports the end of the lower rail, bolted on the outside of the 2 in. x 6 in. *(38 mm x 140 mm)*, with one bolt through the upper end and rail. See Fig. 1.

Bolt the back pieces together in a similar manner with the 2 in. x 6 in. *(38 mm x 140 mm)* ends flush with the 2 in. x 4 in. *(38 mm x 89 mm)* on the ends, and the 1 in. x 2 in. *(17 mm x 38 mm)* piece in place. Attach the end pieces of 2 in. x 6 in. *(38 mm x 140 mm)* as in **FIGURE 3**, with two lag bolts per 2 in. x 6 in. *(38 mm x 140 mm)* end; the lag bolts go into the corner posts. You will need a 5/32 in. *(3 mm)* drill bit for the lag-bolt pilot holes. Countersink the heads flush with a ¾ in. *(20 mm)* bit or leave them above the surface as you wish.

Mark and drill the holes for the dowels and the guard-rails for the ends as before, and fasten in place.

Fasten the 1 in. x 2 in. *(17 mm x 38 mm)* pieces at the ends, flush with the bottom edges of the 2 in. x 6 in. *(38 mm x 140 mm)*, and attach with the flat-head wood screws. Set some screws along the longer pieces of 1 in. x 2 in. *(17 mm x 38 mm)* along the sides.

Cut the sheets of particle board or chipboard to the inside dimensions of the frame so that they rest on the 1 in. x 2 in. *(17 mm x 38 mm)*. They should be cut about 35¾ in. x 71¾ in. *(905 mm x 1820 mm)* to allow some space to drop them in place. If the frame is not quite square, but the above pieces are cut square, force the frame until the pieces drop in place.

If some of the dowels, especially the ladder rungs, are loose in their holes and turn, secure them by setting a nail into them from the sides of the 2 in. x 2 in. *(38 mm x 38 mm)* or 2 in. x 4 in. *(38 mm x 89 mm)*. This is especially important for the ladder rungs, because a turning dowel could cause a child to fall while climbing to the top bunk.

25

Sandbox

Since toddlers love playing in the sand, a sandbox in the backyard is a great idea. In Penny's second year, as soon as the weather began to get warm, I made her a sandbox in which she amused herself for hours on end.

Sand is available at building supply stores at low cost. It is washed sand for making mortar and is free of debris. Two or three bags is a sufficient amount.

I made a cover for Penny's sandbox to help keep the sand dry when it rained and also to prevent fouling by unwelcome deposits from neighborhood cats and dogs.

What You Need

TOOLS: saw, miter box and saw, hammer, measuring tape

MATERIALS:

3/8 in. *(10 mm)* chipboard
- ☐ one sheet 4 ft. x 8 ft. *(1200 mm x 2400 mm)*

1 in. x 2 in. *(17 mm x 38 mm)* softwood
- ☐ seven pieces 8 ft. *(2400 mm)*

- ☐ 1 in. *(25 mm)* common nails (with a head)
- ☐ 1½ in. *(40 mm)* finishing nails
- ☐ *optional: 4 ft. x 4 ft.* (1200 mm x 1200 mm) *chipboard for the cover*

FIG. 1

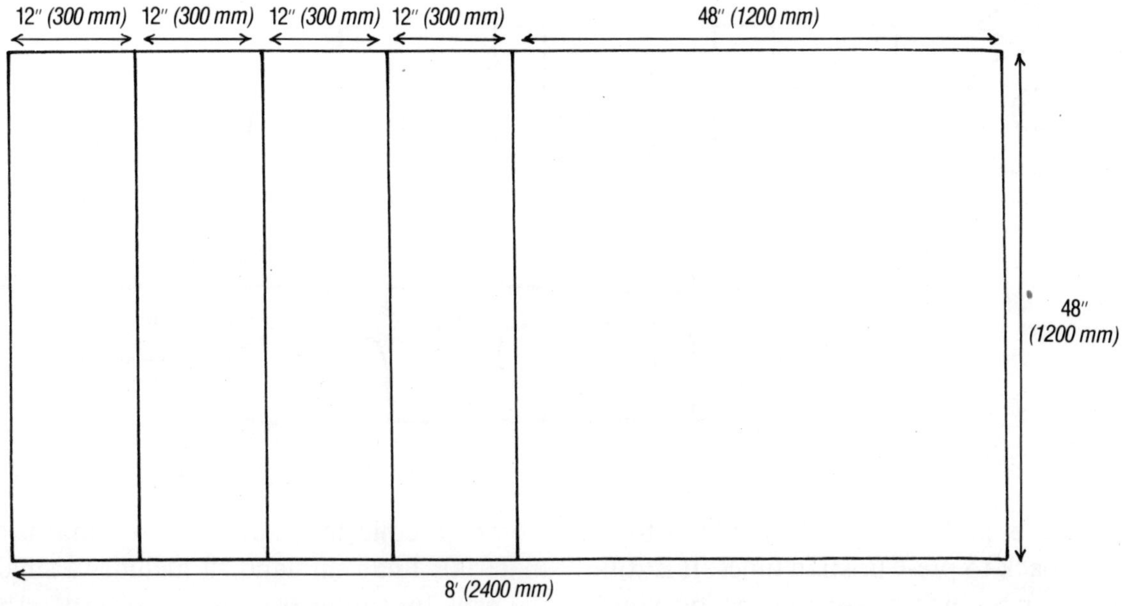

FIG. 2

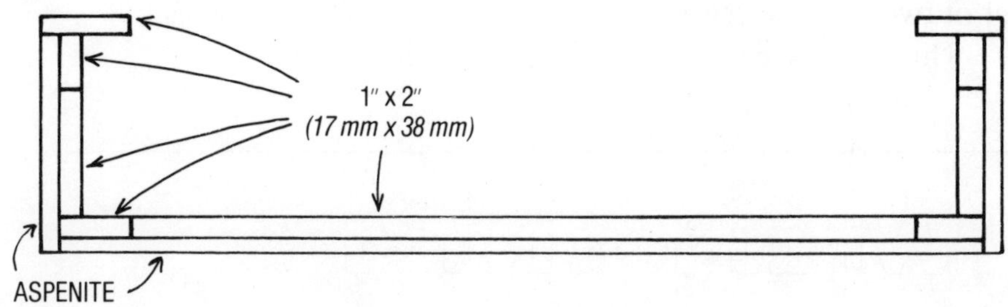

Building Instructions

Cut the sheet of chipboard as in **FIGURE 1**. Plywood could be used as well, but chipboard is less expensive.

Cut pieces of 1 in. x 2 in. *(17 mm x 38 mm)* to go around the edges of the 4 ft. x 4 ft. *(1200 mm x 1200 mm)* bottom piece so that the 1 in. x 2 in. *(17 mm x 38 mm)* will be flush with the outer edges. The corners can be either butt joints or mitered as you wish. The 1 in. x 2 in. *(17 mm x 38 mm)* should be lying flat as in **FIGURE 2**; nail on with 1 in. *(25 mm)* nails every 8 in. *(200 mm)* through the chipboard into the 1 in. x 2 in. *(17 mm x 38 mm)*.

Cut two pieces of 1 in. x 2 in. *(17 mm x 38 mm)* 4 ft. *(1200 mm)* long and nail each along two opposite side pieces flush with the top edge. Cut four pieces of 1 in. x 2 in. *(17 mm x 38 mm)* 9¼ in. *(245 mm)* long and nail these flush with the ends of the side pieces, butted against the 1 in. x 2 in. *(17 mm x 38 mm)* pieces that you nailed to the top edge.

Set these two side pieces against two sides of the bottom piece with the 1 in. x 2 in. *(17 mm x 38 mm)* up (see **FIGURE 2**) and nail them in place. Nail the other side pieces in place with nails going into the corner pieces and the 1 in. x 2 in. *(17 mm x 38 mm)* along the bottom piece. Note that the corners will not overlap but will be open to the corner post.

Measure the length of the 1 in. x 2 in. *(17 mm x 38 mm)* you will need to go across the top of the latter two side pieces, and nail in place.

Now nail on the rails around the top edge that will cover the upper edge of the chipboard and the upper 1 in. x 2 in. *(17 mm x 38 mm)*. Miter these corners and nail in place with the 1½ in. *(40 mm)* finishing nails.

The cover is made by nailing a piece of 1 in. x 2 in. *(17 mm x 38 mm)* across the middle of the 4 ft. x 4 ft. *(1200 mm x 1200 mm)* piece. When putting the top on, weigh down each corner with a brick or stone.

Sand the rough places and apply two coats of oil-base stain, or leave unfinished as I did.

26 Hobbyhorse

The hobbyhorse is perhaps one of the oldest toys known, dating back to pre-Christian times. It is still popular and will be greatly appreciated by your running, jumping and never-standing-still youngster of two to three years.

This toy is easily built from odd pieces of wood; I collected some scraps and used what materials I had on hand. It includes a small box at the back for toting around a favorite plaything such as a teddy bear. The end is supported by a single wheel.

What You Need

TOOLS: saw, square, saber saw, drill and bits, hammer, screwdriver, hole saw

MATERIALS:

¾ in. *(18 mm)* plywood
- ☐ one piece 5 in. x 38 in. *(27 mm x 965 mm)*

½ in. *(12 mm)* plywood
- ☐ one piece 6 in. x 10 in. *(152 mm x 254 mm)*
- ☐ one piece 7 in. x 8 in. *(178 mm x 203 mm)*
- ☐ one piece 3½ in. x 6 in. *(88 mm x 152 mm)*

scrap to make a 2½ in. *(63 mm)* wheel

½ in. *(12 mm)* or ¾ in. *(20 mm)* dowels
- ☐ one 2 in. *(50 mm)* for wheel axle
- ☐ one 7 in. *(178 mm)* for handle

quarter round
- ☐ two pieces 5 in. *(127 mm)*

wood screws
- ☐ two 1 in. *(25 mm)* No. 6 flat-head wood screws

☐ 1¼ in. *(32 mm)* finishing nails

☐ 1½ in. *(40 mm)* finishing nails

☐ glue

☐ ¼ in. *(6 mm)* cord for reins, 30 in. *(760 mm)* long

FIG. 1

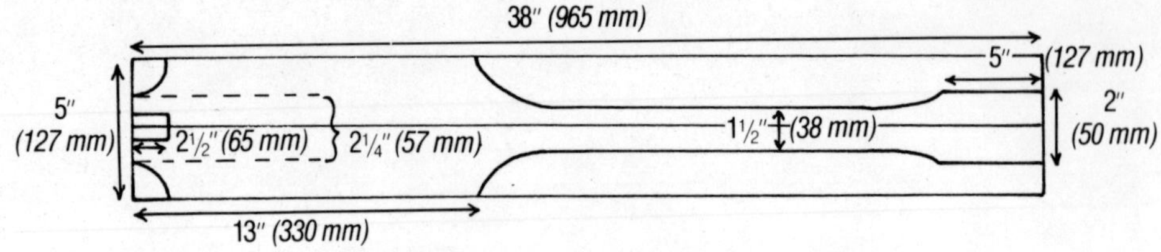

FIG. 2

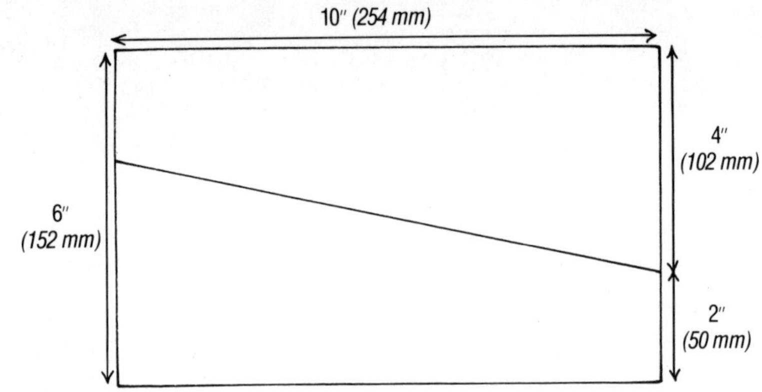

Building Instructions

Begin by cutting the ¾ in. *(18 mm)* piece of plywood as in **FIGURE 1**. The slot at one end is for the wheel, so make it about ⅛ in. *(3 mm)* wider than the wheel. Shape the corners as in **FIGURE 1**, using any pleasing shape. The cutting is easily done with a saber saw.

Cut the sides for the box from the 6 in. x 10 in. *(152 mm x 254 mm)* piece of plywood as in **FIGURE 2**, and nail and glue these pieces to the edges of the ¾ in. *(18 mm)* plywood base with the back end 3 in. *(75 mm)* from the end.

The 3½ in. x 6 in. *(88 mm x 152 mm)* piece of plywood makes the end of the box. Nail and glue it to the back edges of the side pieces.

Cut the horse's head out of the 7 in. x 8 in. *(178 mm x 203 mm)* piece of plywood, but locate the hole for the dowel handle beforehand. I drew the head freehand because only the basic shape is required. If need be you can plot out **FIGURE 3** into squares to help you draw the head. Do not make the ears come to too sharp a point.

Cut the two 5 in. *(127 mm)* pieces of quarter round, and nail and glue them with the horse's head sandwiched between them at the part of the plywood that's 2 in. *(50 mm)* wide. Some of the nails should go directly into the plywood base while others cross through the base of the horse's neck. The forward end of the neck should be flush with the end of the plywood base.

Using your drill and hole saw with the 2½ in. *(63 mm)* diameter cutter, make the wheel from a scrap piece of plywood. Remember that the wheel will be neater if you cut first from one side partway through, then turn over the wood and complete the cutting from the other side.

Make the hole for the axle slightly bigger than the diameter of your axle dowel, ⅝ in. *(15 mm)* for the ½ in. *(12 mm)* dowel, or ⅞ in. *(22 mm)* for the ¾ in. *(20 mm)* dowel. Slide the wheel onto the dowel and fit it into place. The wheel should turn easily and not touch the box end or the end of the slot. Using your square, check to be sure that the dowel is straight across, and clamp one end of the dowel in place while drilling the countersink, pilot and shank holes for the screws. When one side is drilled, fit the screw after putting a dab of glue between the dowel and plywood. Then clamp, drill, glue and set the other screw. Note that if you are using a softwood dowel the grain of the wood should be at right angles to the screw.

Fit the dowel in the horse's neck for the handle; then set a nail in from the edge of the plywood into the dowel to help hold it in place. Your efforts should now look like **FIGURE 4**.

Finish and paint as desired, but be careful when painting around the wheel, since too much paint might make it stick to the axle and prevent it from turning.

FIG. 3

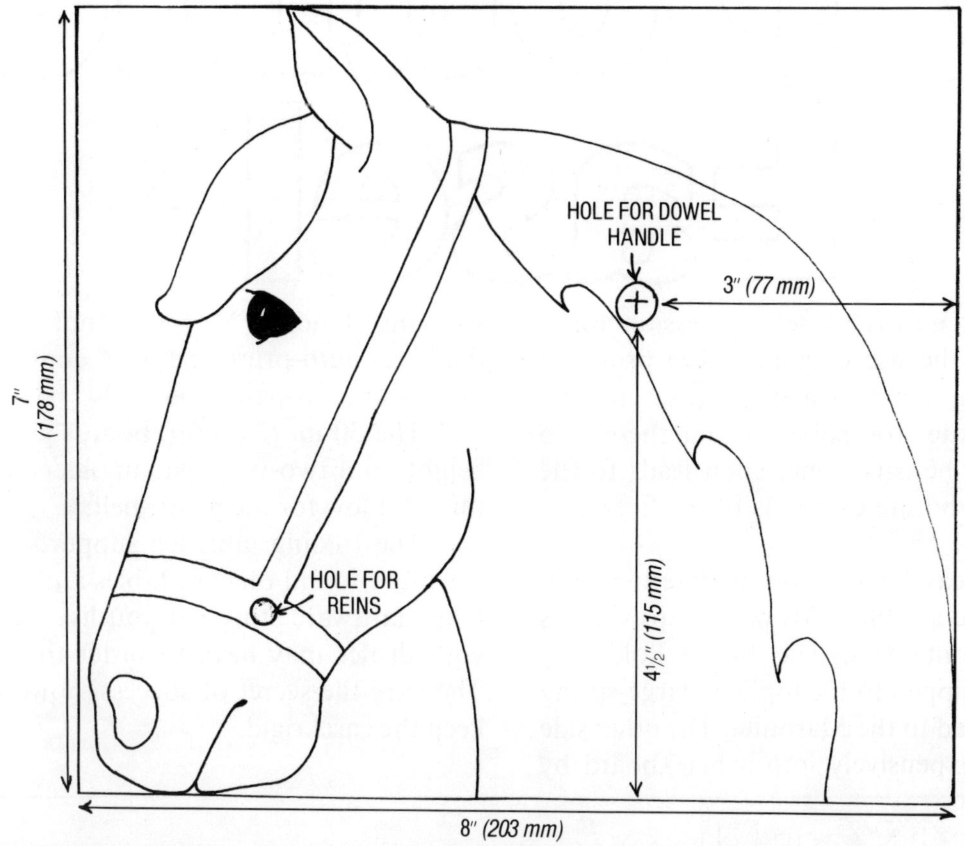
HOLE FOR DOWEL HANDLE
3″ (77 mm)
7″ (178 mm)
4½″ (115 mm)
HOLE FOR REINS
8″ (203 mm)

FIG. 4

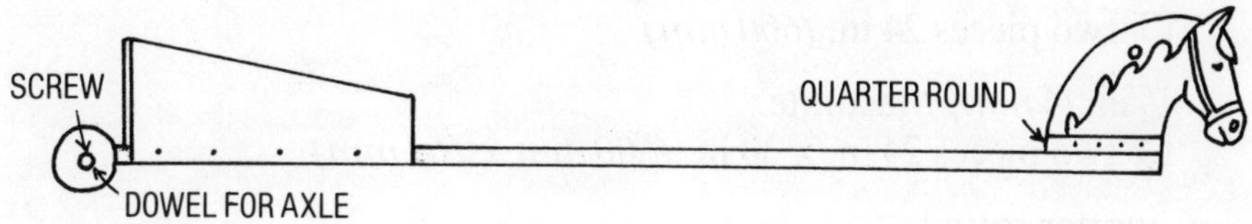
SCREW
QUARTER ROUND
DOWEL FOR AXLE

27 Double Easel

One of the best means of self-expression for a growing child is the use of paints. The primitive finger painting of the two-year-old (use custard, especially chocolate, for paint so that there's no need to worry if he eats some) soon leads to the comparatively elaborate creations of the five-year-old.

The double easel can accommodate two children. On one side a shelf holds paint cups such as plastic yogurt containers. The board holds the paper, which is clipped to the top with large-spring paper clips or taped to the Masonite. The other side can be made inexpensively into a blackboard by spraying standard Masonite (not oil treated) with flat black auto-primer paint. A conventional brush-on blackboard paint could also be used.

The 30 in. *(762 mm)* boards give a reasonable height for a two-year-old; an older child might find this a bit low for the paint shelf.

The folding table-leg supports are those that are often found on card tables and are available at large hardware stores. If you live in a small town, your dealer may have to order this item for you. They are the secret of success, however, since they keep the easel rigid.

What You Need

TOOLS: saw, measuring tape, miter box and saw, drill and bits, screwdriver, hole saw for drill

MATERIALS:

1 in. x 2 in. *(17 mm x 38 mm)* pine, spruce or fir
- ☐ four pieces 48 in. *(1220 mm)*

1 in. x 4 in. *(17 mm x 89 mm)* pine or fir
- ☐ two pieces 24 in. *(600 mm)*

¼ in. *(6 mm)* Masonite
- ☐ two pieces 24 in. x 30 in. *(600 mm x 762 mm)*

quarter round
- ☐ one piece 36 in. *(1000 mm)*

- ☐ one pair 3 in. *(75 mm)* strap hinges with screws for same
- ☐ two folding leg supports, one right-handed, one left-handed
- ☐ six 2 in. *(50 mm)* No. 8 round-head wood screws
- ☐ ten ¼ in. *(6 mm)* flat washers
- ☐ four ¾ in. *(20 mm)* No. 8 round-head wood screws
- ☐ 1 in. *(25 mm)* finishing nails
- ☐ glue

FIG. 1

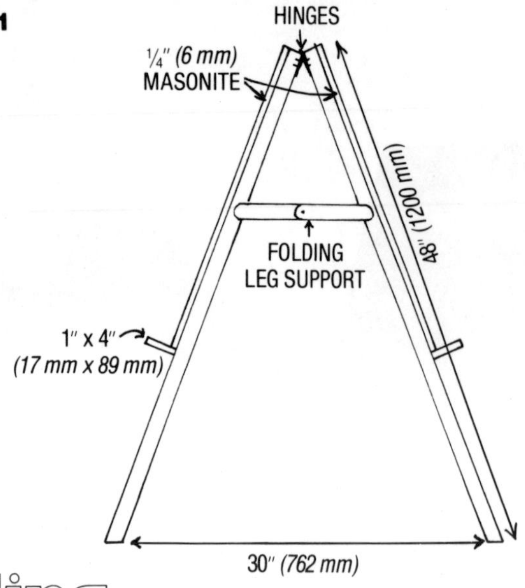

FIG. 2

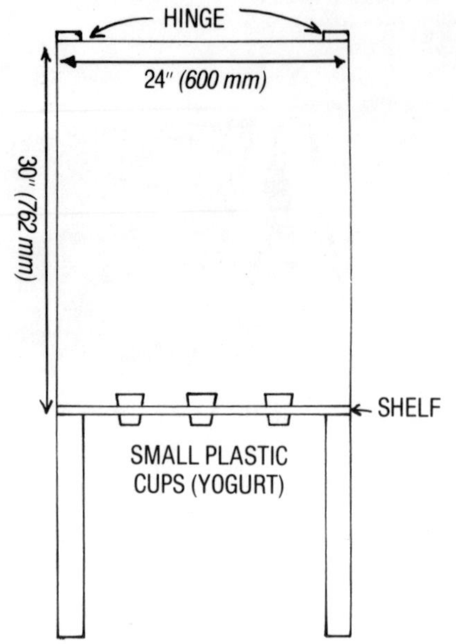

Building Instructions

Cut the 1 in. x 2 in. *(17 mm x 38 mm)* to length and the Masonite to size. Glue and nail the Masonite to the 1 in. x 2 in. *(17 mm x 38 mm)*, keeping the edges of the Masonite flush with one end of the 1 in. x 2 in. *(17 mm x 38 mm)* and with the sides of the 1 in. x 2 in. *(17 mm x 38 mm)*. Lay the rough side of the Masonite against the 1 in. x 2 in. *(17 mm x 38 mm)*.

Lay the two pieces out flat with the Masonite down and the 1 in. x 2 in. *(17 mm x 38 mm)* almost touching, and attach the hinges with the screws.

The folding leg supports will probably require adjustment—at least, the ones I bought could not fold up as made. Both ends of the folding leg supports must be flat, and must be able to take a screw. Mine had a plate for two screws riveted to one end; I simply removed the rivet, using a ¼ in. *(6 mm)* bit and drilling from the dimpled end of the rivet, then detached and discarded the plate.

Open the legs of the easel about 30 in. *(762 mm)* and locate the spot where the folding leg supports, when locked straight, will fit at the side of the 1 in. x 2 in. *(17 mm x 38 mm)*. (See **FIGURE 1**.) Mark the place for the screw pilot holes. Close the legs to check if the holes are beside each other with the legs together. If the holes are not the same distance from the top, the legs will not fold properly. The screw holes for my leg supports were about 13 in. *(330 mm)* from the top.

One end of the folding leg support will be attached flat to the 1 in. x 2 in. *(17 mm x 38 mm)* while the other end must be set off the opposite 1 in. x 2 in. *(17 mm x 38 mm)* leg. The flat washers are there for spacers, so use the right thickness. I needed five flat washers per side. Attach the side with the flat washers with one 2 in. *(50 mm)* No. 8 round-head wood screw.

Decide what size containers you will be using for the paints. I used the 175 g yogurt cups with closeable lids. I made the holes in one of the shelves—the 1 in. x 4 in. x 24 in. *(17 mm x 89 mm x 600 mm)*—to accommodate three. The holes I made were 2½ in. *(63 mm)* in diameter, which is the largest-size cutter for my hole saw. I centered the three cup holes along the shelf about 1 in. *(25 mm)* apart.

Attach the shelf along the bottom edge of one of the Masonite sides. It should be over the lower end so that two of the shorter screws can go into it through the Masonite. Use one of the 2 in. *(50 mm)* No. 8 screws to go through the leg into the shelf at each end.

I painted the other side with three coats of the blackboard paint. Sand the Masonite surface lightly with fine sandpaper first and wipe off the dust. Let the paint harden for at least twenty-four hours. An unpainted Masonite surface can also act as a blackboard, but it is not as good as one prepared in the above manner.

The shelf for the blackboard side has its outer three sides lined with the quarter round to help keep the chalk and erasers on it. The flat side of the quarter round should be on the inside. Miter the corners. Attach this shelf in the same way as the other after you have painted the blackboard on.

I did not finish the wood, but sanded the rough areas.

28

Playhouse Panels

Children love playing house and will do so in any slightly enclosed space. Panels of ¼ in. *(6 mm)* Masonite with 1 in. x 2 in. *(17 mm x 38 mm)* softwood strapping glued and nailed around the perimeter creates a simple, durable playhouse that can be folded flat for storage.

A screen 30 in. *(760 mm)* high enables a two-year-old to peek over the top. A screen 48 in. *(1200 mm)* high with three sides, as illustrated in **FIGURE 1**, makes an inviting, partially enclosed area for play. The addition of a window in the center panel allows the children to play store. A rope from either side will hold up a hinged shelf.

A four-sided house with a roof can also be made to dismantle with removable pin hinges. If some of the pins from the hinges are lost, simply file the point off a nail with a head and use as a replacement pin.

For a playhouse that is to be set up outdoors, be sure to use oil-treated Masonite. All windows and doors should be framed with the 1 in. x 2 in. *(17 mm x 38 mm)* to make the openings more durable.

What You Need

TOOLS: saw, square, hammer, miter box, tape measure, screwdriver

MATERIALS:

¼ in. *(6 mm)* Masonite
- ☐ one sheet 4 ft. x 8 ft. *(1200 mm x 2400 mm)*

1 in. x 2 in. *(17 mm x 38 mm)* softwood (pine or spruce)
- ☐ five pieces 8 ft. *(2400 mm)*
- ☐ two pairs 1 in. x 2 in. *(25 mm x 50 mm)* hinges with screws for same
- ☐ ¾ in. *(20 mm)* finishing nails
- ☐ glue

FIG. 1

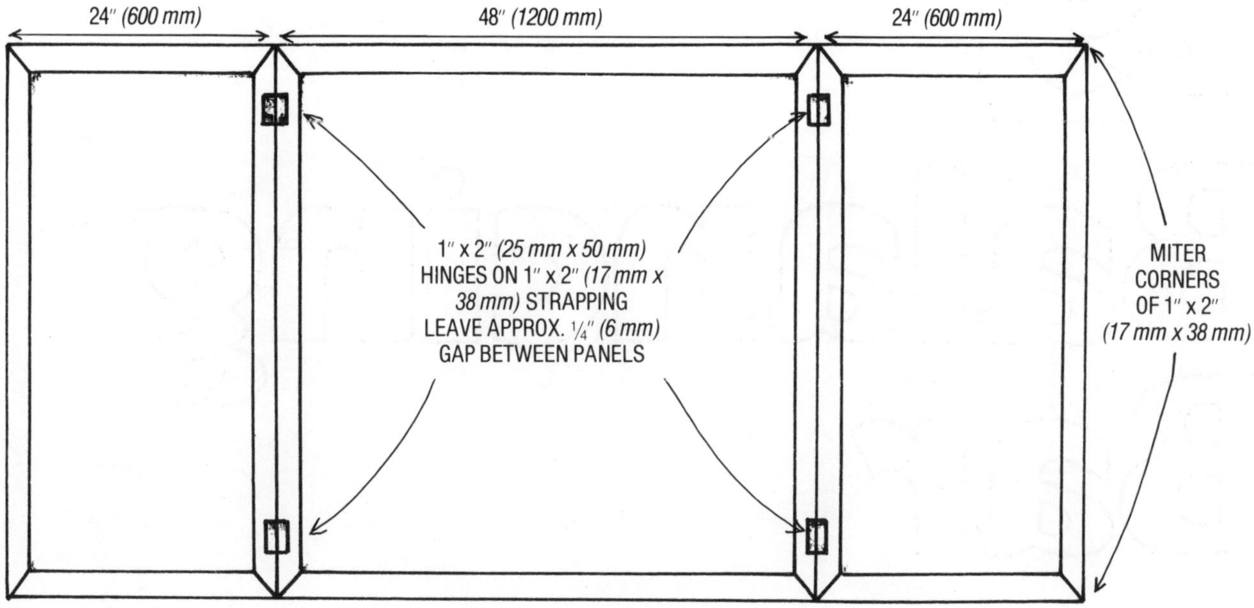

1″ x 2″ *(17 mm x 38 mm)* STRAPPING ALL AROUND
THREE PANELS GLUED AND NAILED TO ROUGH
SIDE OF MASONITE

Building Instructions

Mitered corners are best on the strapping, although a butt joint at the corners is acceptable. For extra strength at the corners a 4 in. *(100 mm)* plywood gusset could be added, but use ⅛ in. *(4 mm)* plywood or Masonite, otherwise the panels will not hinge flat for storage.

I have made several of these panels for various purposes and have always been surprised at how strong and long-lasting they are. The panel in the photograph was made using Peg Board.

One disadvantage is that if a panel is knocked flat and walked on by heavy children, the Masonite could tear. If you should be so unlucky as to have this happen, get another sheet of Masonite and nail it over the damaged one. It will be heavier but stronger.

If you want a more attractive screen, perhaps for use as a room divider to section off a study area, get two sheets of Masonite (or plywood wall paneling) and nail one on either side of the 1 in. x 2 in. *(17 mm x 38 mm)*. The panels will then be flush on both sides.

Once you have the panels framed with the 1 in. x 2 in. *(17 mm x 38 mm)* you must decide on which side to put the hinges. I put the hinges on the strapping side, which means that when the panels are opened, the flush side is on the outside with the strapping on the inside.

A variation would be to halve the Masonite sheet into two squares. These would have the 1 in. x 2 in. *(17 mm x 38 mm)* glued and nailed as above with one set of hinges, resulting in a two-sided corner instead of a three-sided panel.

29

Balancing Bar

Children more than two years find it fascinating to test their balance, and this easily built balancing bar gives the child that opportunity. An excellent playground toy, it allows several children to play Follow the Leader, Over the Bar and other such games. It is shown as being 6 ft. *(1800 mm)* long; although a shorter bar could be made, anything shorter than 4 ft. *(1200 mm)* would not be very challenging.

What You Need

TOOLS: saw, square, measuring tape, drill and bits

MATERIALS: 2 in. x 4 in. *(38 mm x 89 mm)* pine, spruce or fir

☐ one piece 8 ft. *(2400 mm)*

☐ two ¼ in. x 4 in. *(6 mm x 100 mm)* carriage bolts and flat washers

7

FIG. 1

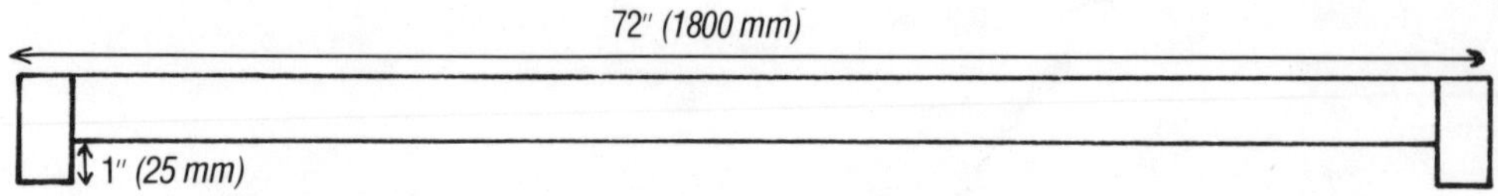

FIG. 2

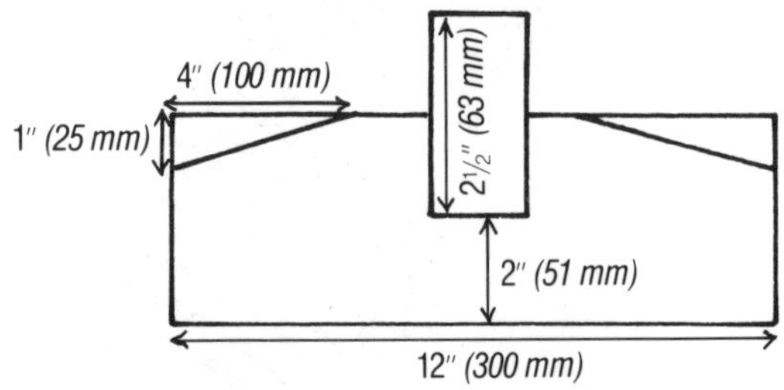

FIG. 3

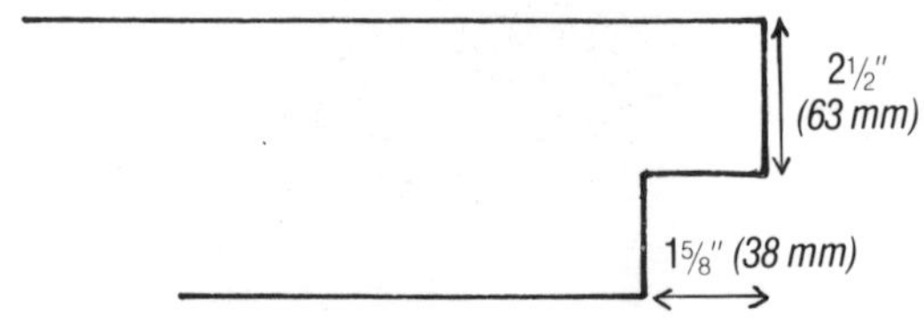

Building Instructions

Cut the 2 in. x 4 in. *(38 mm x 89 mm)* into three pieces: two 12 in. *(300 mm)* long, one 72 in. *(1800 mm)* long. Cut the ends of the 72 in. *(1800 mm)* piece as in **FIGURE 2**, then notch the 12 in. *(300 mm)* pieces as in **FIGURE 3**. When the pieces slot into each other, drill a countersink hole ¾ in. *(18 mm)* in diameter about ⅜ in. *(10 mm)* deep at both top and bottom. Then drill a ¼ in. *(6 mm)* hole for the bolt through the two pieces.

Your drill will be too short to go all the way through, so drill down from the top as deep as possible. The drill should be long enough to partially penetrate the lower piece. Remove the upper piece and complete the hole.

Cut off the corners of the end pieces as in **FIGURE 3**, then bolt the two pieces together.

Sand and smooth the pieces to reduce the possibility of splinters. Leave unpainted, or give the bar a coat of oil-base stain so that the surface will not be slippery.

30 Stilts

Walking stilts have been a favored toy for generations. Not only do they provide an excellent and enjoyable form of exercise for the young child, but they also help in developing a sense of balance.

The crutch tips can be purchased at a surgical supply store or in the cane section of a department store. Ask for tips in the 1 in. *(25 mm)* size, although ⅞ in. *(20 mm)* will do.

What You Need

TOOLS: saw, square, drill and 1 in. *(25 mm)* bit (or expansive bit), hammer

MATERIALS:

½ in. *(12 mm)* plywood
- ☐ two pieces 4½ in. x 5 in. *(114 mm x 127 mm)*
- ☐ two pieces 2 in. x 5 in. *(50 mm x 127 mm)*

1 in. *(25 mm)* hardwood dowels
- ☐ two 48 in. *(1220 mm)*

- ☐ one pair 1 in. *(25 mm)* rubber crutch tips
- ☐ 1¼ in. *(32 mm)* finishing nails
- ☐ glue

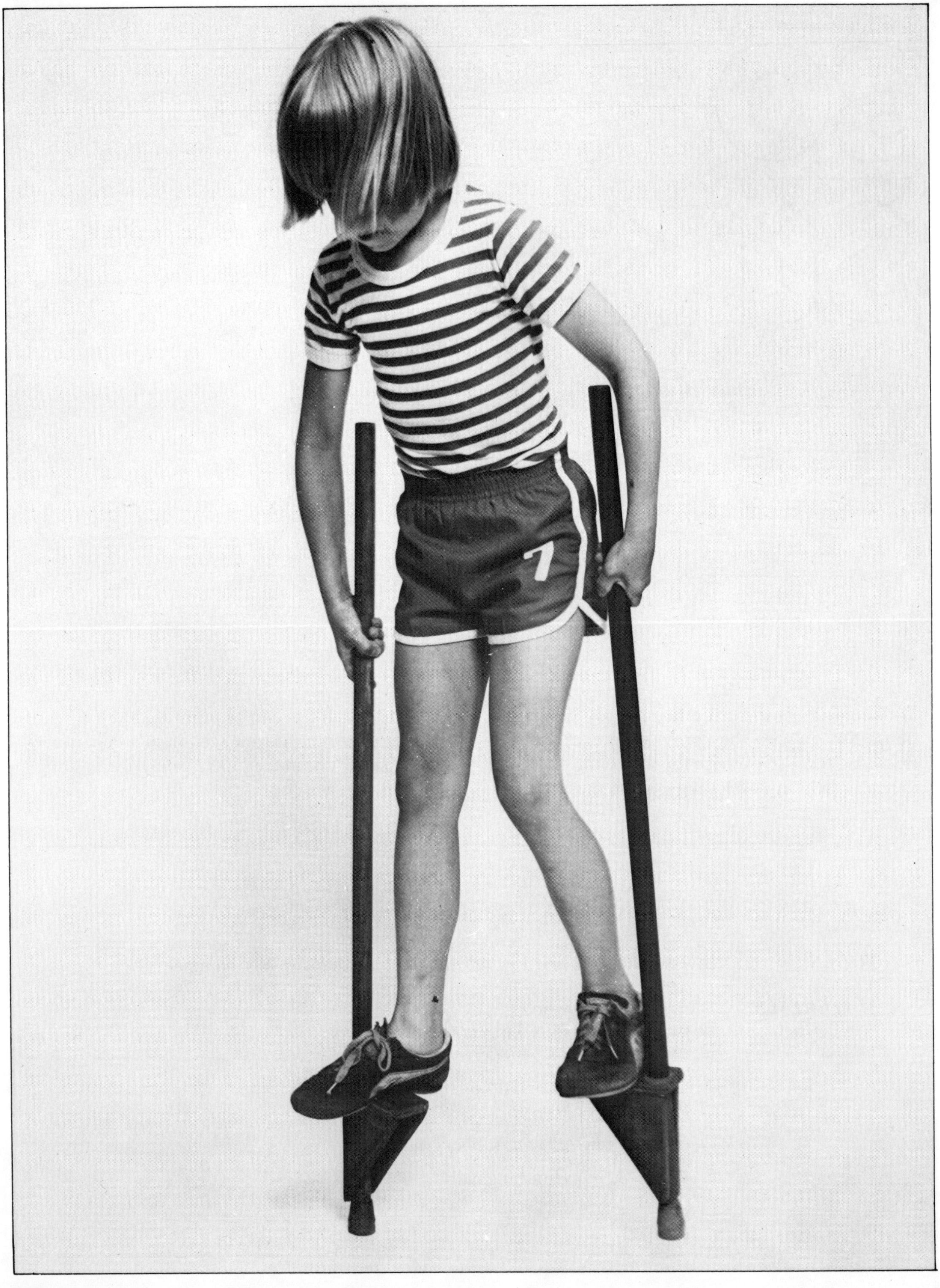
7

FIG. 1

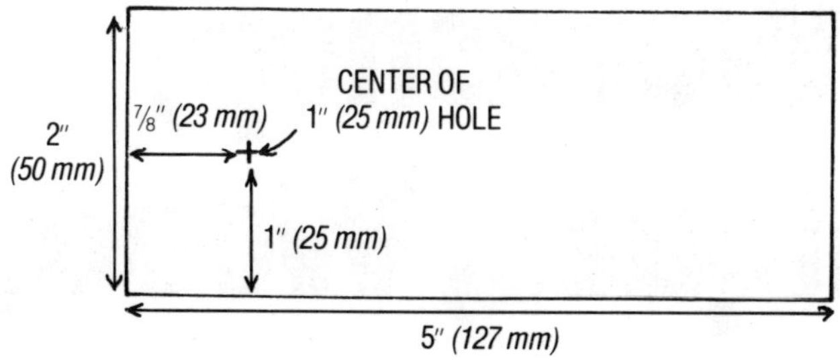

FIG. 2

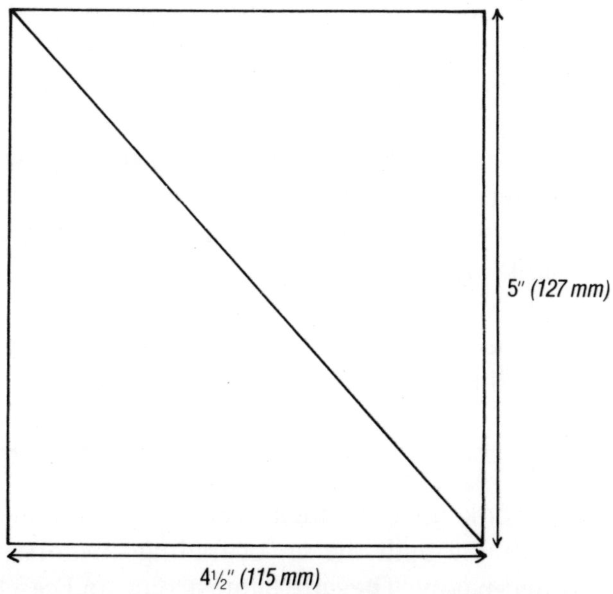

FIG. 3

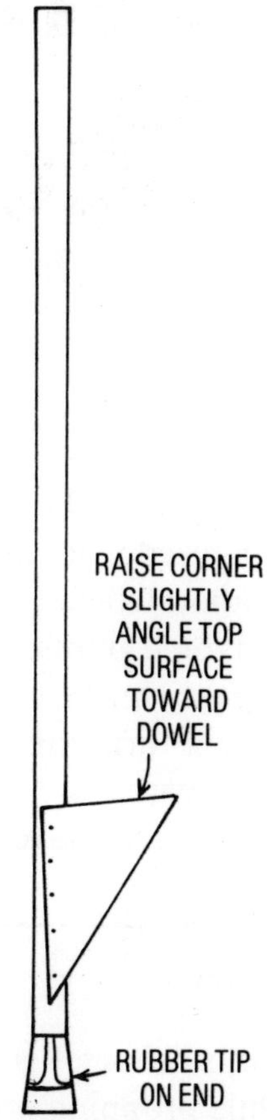

Building Instructions

Begin by cutting the 2 in. x 5 in. *(50 mm x 127 mm)* pieces of plywood and drilling a hole in each, as in **FIGURE 1**.

Cut the 4½ in. x 5 in. *(114 mm x 127 mm)* plywood rectangles. Then cut them diagonally as in **FIGURE 2**. Cut the dowels to length.

Fit the rubber crutch tips onto one end of the dowels. Although I was told that 1 in. *(25 mm)* tips were available, I could find only the ⅞ in. *(20 mm)* size; to accommodate them I slightly narrowed the tips of the dowels with my Surform file and sanded them smooth. When the rubber tips fit, mark where their upper ends fit on the dowels and then remove them.

Dab some glue on the edge of the dowel above the mark for the upper end of the tip and nail one of the triangular pieces in place with the 5 in. *(127 mm)* side of the triangle lying along the dowel. Put these pieces on a slight angle so that when the top piece is nailed in place it will angle slightly toward the dowel. This helps keep little feet from sliding off. (See **FIGURE 3**.)

When one piece is nailed to the dowel, turn the dowel over and nail the opposite side on in the same manner, but be sure it parallels the first in all respects.

To nail the foot piece in place, start two nails on each side, slide it on over the dowel, dab a bit of glue onto the upper surface of the triangular pieces and nail in place. This is the hardest piece to nail in place because you must hold the stilt upright and nail into a relatively unsupported piece. Get someone to help hold the pieces, and strike the nails with light blows; if you don't, you could knock the whole thing apart.

Round the corners and finish as desired. The final step is to put the rubber tips back on.

Part III / Workshop, Techniques, Wood, Tools

Basics

Before you begin working on the projects in this book, an organized work area is essential. This need not be the elaborate workshop often pictured in the various handyman publications; a small and compact work space can be equally functional.

I have built furniture in various settings, often cramped areas with only a minimum of space and tools. My work areas have ranged from a cluttered back room, to the front hallway of a twenty-fourth-floor apartment in a high-rise building, to my present corner in the basement.

The basic needs are: a surface on which to lay the wood while marking and cutting it (sawhorses are recommended); a surface on which to lay the pieces while assembling them (a workbench, a spare plank laying across your sawhorses, or the floor); and a warm, dry area in which the articles you make can be painted. If it matters, surrounding areas should be protected from paint splatters.

SAWHORSES

A good set of sawhorses is a necessity. I have built furniture while propping boards on chairs, benches and other such surfaces, but working in this fashion can be frustrating. If the boards are not lying flat, your cuts are unlikely to be straight or square.

My first set of sawhorses was made with the brackets that can be found at a hardware store. These sawhorses were wobbly and unacceptable. The second set, nailed together, was good and solid but took up too much space when not in use. I eventually built the set of folding sawhorses illustrated below. They are light, strong, and can be put away when not needed. They are ready for work at a moment's notice, and I would have no others.

Use 1 in. x 6 in. *(17 mm x 140 mm)* softwood for a light pair of sawhorses, or 2 in. x 4 in. *(38 mm x 89 mm)* for a heavier set. Note that you will need longer screws and nails if using wood that is 2 in. *(38 mm)* thick.

What You Need

TOOLS: saw, square, hammer, drill and bits for the screw pilot holes, screwdriver

MATERIALS:

1 in. x 6 in. *(17 mm x 140 mm)* softwood
- ☐ twelve pieces 30 in. *(760 mm)*

1 in. x 2 in. *(17 mm x 38 mm)* softwood
- ☐ four pieces 39 in. *(990 mm)*
- ☐ two pairs of 4 in. *(100 mm)* strap hinges
- ☐ twenty-four 1½ in. *(35 mm)* No. 8 flat-head wood screws
- ☐ glue
- ☐ two pieces of rope—anything approx. ½ in. *(12 mm)* in diameter and 54 in. *(1370 mm)* long

Building Instructions

Cut all the wood to length, but be sure that it has no large knots, which could weaken it.

Lay out three 30 in. *(760 mm)* pieces as in **FIGURE 1** with the crosspiece and brace lying on top of the legs. Smear some glue on the boards where they cross, check to see that they are square, and nail them in place. Glue and nail the 1 in. x 2 in. *(17 mm x 38 mm)* in the same manner, cutting the angles now or later.

Make all four pieces in the same way. When they are matched in pairs, the supports will criss-cross each other.

Attach the hinges as in **FIGURE 2** so that they are lying on the legs, not the cross supports. There should be a slight opening between the two frames: ¼ in. *(6 mm)* will do.

Drill pilot holes for the screws to prevent the board from splitting.

Stand the sawhorses up with the legs together and loop the rope around the two braces, tying a square knot a few inches from the rope ends.

The height of the crosspieces can be adjusted by lengthening or shortening the rope, although the wider the legs are spread, the more they will flex when heavily loaded.

Sawhorses

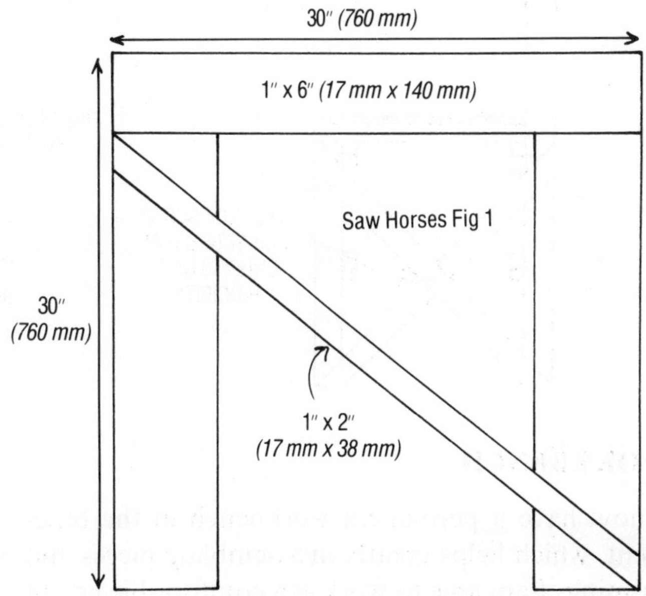

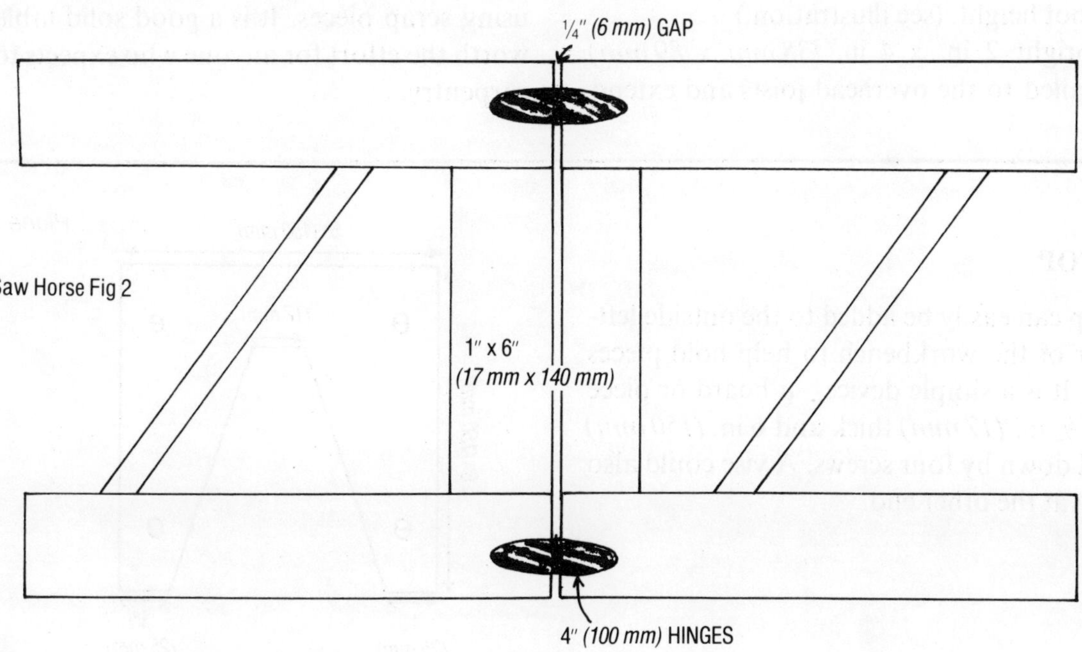

Workbench End and Front View

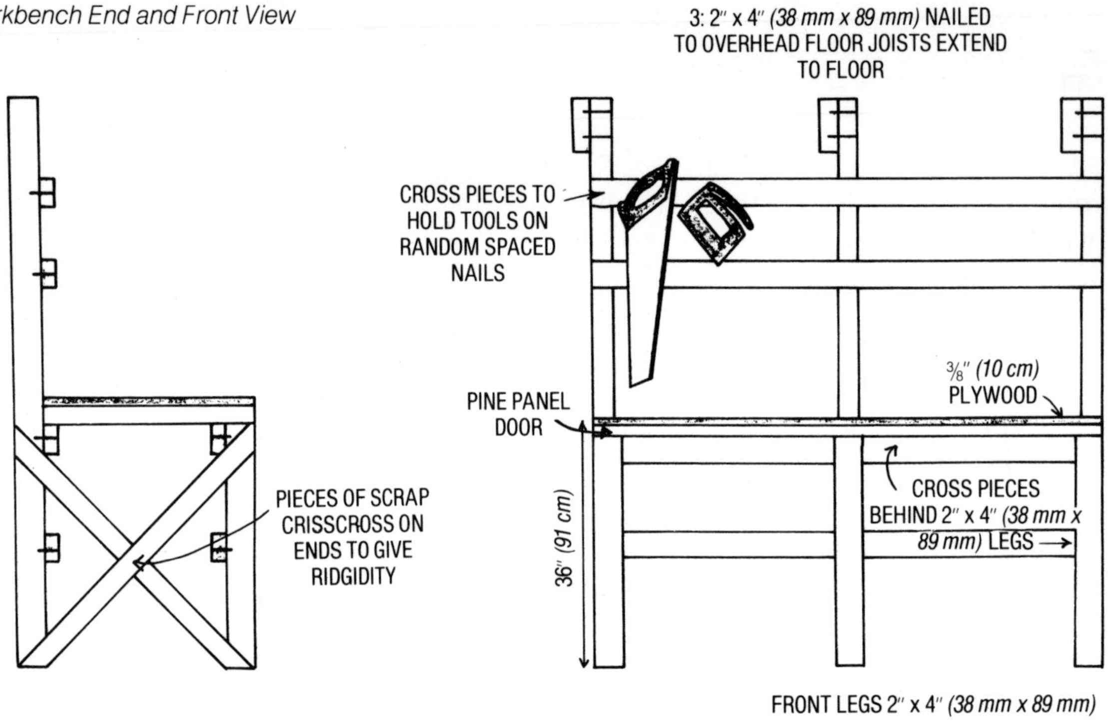

WORKBENCH

I now have a permanent workbench in the basement, which helps greatly in assembling pieces and painting. I am able to work at a comfortable height and can leave things where they lie for long periods of time.

My workbench consists of an old interior pine panel door 32 in. x 94 in. *(810 mm x 2400 mm)*, with a piece of plywood ⅜ in. *(10 mm)* thick glued and nailed in place to cover the top surface. Its upper surface is 36 in. *(92 cm)* from the floor, about right for my six-foot height. (see illustration.)

The upright 2 in. x 4 in. *(38 mm x 89 mm)* pieces are nailed to the overhead joists and extend down to the floor. The front legs are 2 in. x 4 in. *(38 mm x 89 mm)* with a cross-piece at the top nailed to the legs. Then the top is nailed to the crosspiece. Another crosspiece goes behind the legs about 15 in. *(380 mm)* above the floor. The crisscross pieces on the ends are scrap pieces of plywood nailed and glued in place for rigidity.

Crosspieces nailed to the back uprights provide lots of space for tools hung on nails. Position the nails to accommodate the various tool shapes.

I built my workbench for next to nothing by using scrap pieces. It is a good solid table and well worth the effort for anyone who expects to do much carpentry.

PLANE STOP

A plane stop can easily be added to the outside left-hand corner of the workbench to help hold pieces for planing. It is a simple device—a board or piece of plywood ¾ in. *(17 mm)* thick and 6 in. *(150 mm)* square, held down by four screws. A vise could also be bolted on at the other end.

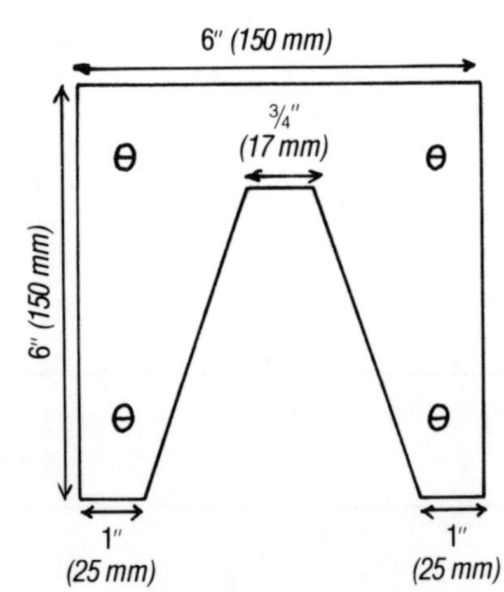

Plane Stop

CLAMPS

Clamps are good tools to have but are expensive to buy. I made my own clamps very economically; they do not have the power of strong metal clamps, but for casual woodworking they are fine for holding boards or clamping things together while glue dries.

Two styles of my homemade clamps are of the duckbill type.

The wedge-type clamps are best cut from 3/4 in. *(20 mm)* plywood and the wedge from 1 in. x 2 in. *(17 mm x 38 mm)* or 2 in. x 2 in. *(38 mm x 38 mm).* Attach the wedge to the clamp by drilling a hole through both pieces and tying them together with cord.

These light-duty clamps are easily made to any size. I cut mine from plywood with my saber saw virtually freehand and have made them with openings from 2 in. *(50 mm)* to 5 in. *(130 mm).* Keep the opening about 5 in. *(130 mm)* deep and the width of the sides at the narrowest part to 1 1/4 in. *(35 mm)* to allow for some springiness, which helps set the clamp.

The bolt-type duckbill clamp is stronger, and more force can be applied. I show drawings for two, both of which I have used extensively. The smaller one is cut from the width of a 2 in. x 4 in. *(38 mm x 89 mm)* with a 1/4 in. *(6 mm)* carriage bolt 4 in. *(10 mm)* long with a flat washer and wing nut.

The second bolt type is also made from 2 in. x 4 in. *(38 mm x 89 mm)*, but the top and bottom pieces are laid flat. The spreader is a piece of 2 in. x 4 in. *(38 mm x 89 mm)* on edge. In mine I have a 3/8 in. *(10 mm)* carriage bolt 8 in. *(200 mm)* long with a flat washer and wing nut. This clamp can hold items up to 5 in. *(130 mm)* thick if slightly hollowed out with the Surform file between the end and the bolt.

For clamping wider objects I use what is called a Spanish windlass. With some strong cord simply make a loop around the pieces you want to clamp. Knot it firmly (I use a bow-line), and insert some buffer blocks between the line and your pieces of wood. Then wind the cord tight using a short piece of dowel. Tuck the dowel under the line, and it will hold itself.

Wedge-Type Duckbill Clamp

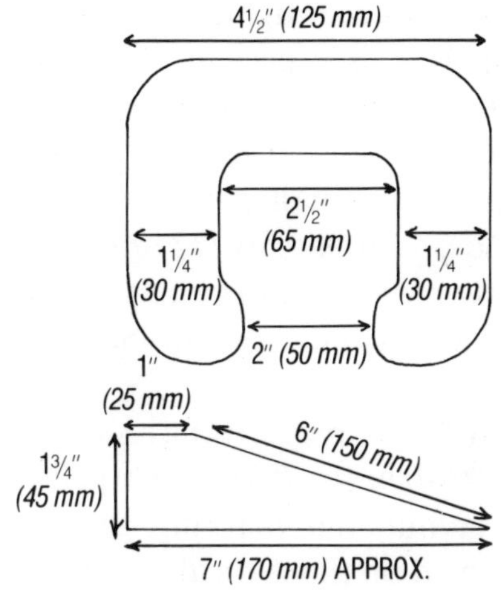

Large Bolt-Type Duckbill Clamp

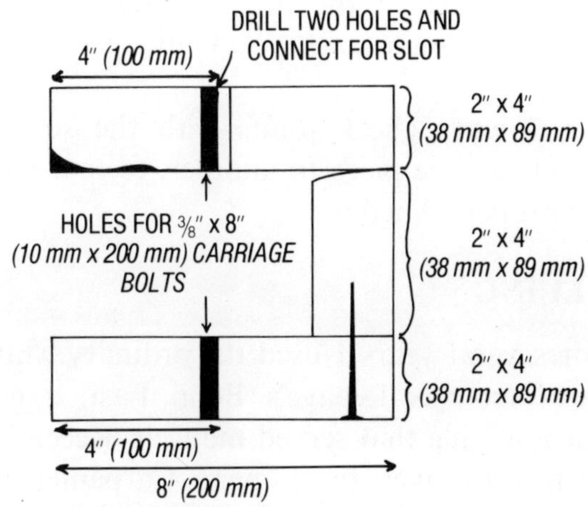

Smaller Bolt-Type Duckbill Clamp

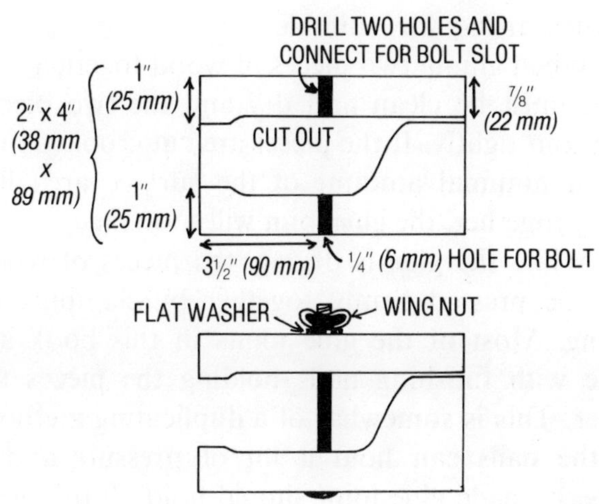

CARPENTRY

One of the most difficult things for the beginning carpenter is to make straight, accurate cuts. When using handsaws it is especially hard—you might make a cut that is not vertical to the surface of the boards, or you might cut diagonally across from edge to edge. For small pieces such as dowels, quarter rounds, ¾ in. x ¾ in. *(17 mm x 17 mm)* and 1 in. x 2 in. *(17 mm x 38 mm)*, a miter box is a great help in making not only straight cuts but also 45° angle cuts.

Mark out larger pieces using a square. I like the 24 in. x 16 in. *(610 mm x 405 mm)* carpenter's square for general layout and marking. A combination square when held on the vertical next to the saw will ensure that the saw is vertical to the surface when you start the cuts.

Another old-time aid for making straight cuts is to clamp a piece of straight 2 in. x 4 in. *(38 mm x 89 mm)* next to the line you want to cut. This provides a guide to let you know when you are out of line.

Always check joints with the square when attaching one piece to another, to make sure they are properly lined up.

GLUING

For several years I used the ordinary white wood glues such as Lepage's Bond Fast, a good all-purpose glue that served me well. Recently I have been won over by Elmer's Carpenter Glue by Borden. It sets faster, holds poorly fitting joints better, and seems more water resistant.

I mention brand names not because I have any connection with the companies but to give the amateur an idea of what to use. I am sure other products are equally suitable.

When gluing two pieces of wood together, the wood must be clean and dry and the two pieces must join tightly. If the pieces are cut crooked and only a minimal amount of the surface area lies tightly together, the glue joint will soon fail.

While the glue is drying, the pieces of wood must be pressed firmly together by clamping or nailing. Most of the glue joints in this book are made with finishing nails holding the pieces together. This is somewhat of a duplicating method, for the nails can hold a lot of pressure and a properly made glue joint should hold all the pressure. But if the glue joint is poor, the nails help it. Always use glue; nails can work loose with heavy use, causing a joint that relies on them to fail.

WOOD JOINTS

The plain butt joint with an interior or an exterior corner post is the most often used joint in this book because it is easy to make, foolproof and very strong.

Examples of the exterior corner-post butts are the end joints on the toy box and the back of the step-up. I use this type of joint whenever I can; it is attractive and at the same time allows the amateur carpenter to hide minor mistakes in the cutting of the wood. If your cuts are not exact, they will not show.

The interior corner-post type of butt joint, used in the back of the walker, allows the overlapping edges of the plywood to show but gives strong support to the corner. As well, it provides a relatively large surface area for the glue. If done properly, with minor imperfections filled, this joint is useful and attractive.

The open doweled miter joint is used for the hanging frames, and the procedure for making it is outlined in the building instructions for that piece. It is a simple joint to make if you have a miter box and electric drill with bits. The drilling of the holes need not be accurately measured (I do it freehand without measuring). The two mitered pieces must be firmly held at 90° to each other if the frame is to be square when finished. The ends of the hole and the dowel should be of equal distance from the corner and glued in place.

Cross-lap and end half-lap joints are used in the construction of the "jail bars" standard crib. With these joints, two pieces of wood, usually of the same dimensions, cross each other while the joint is kept to the dimensions of one of the pieces. If these joints are to be glued, they must be accurately cut. I show the joints held together with bolts, which allow the crib to be taken apart.

The joint is made by cutting away half the thickness of each of the pieces of wood where they cross, to the width of the crossing piece. Make the cuts at the proper width, then one or two more cuts in between these, and clear the wood with your chisel. The pieces can then be fitted together with their top and bottom surfaces flush with each other.

The final type of joint is the mortise and tenon. I used a pinned-open mortise and tenon joint on the "jail bars" standard crib.

To make the mortise, drill a hole at each end of the mortise the same width that the mortise is to be. Then clean out the wood between the holes and make the corners square with a sharp chisel. Accuracy is very important. (See illustration.)

The tenon is made by cutting away a quarter of the total width of the wood from each side. Cut in from the end to the depth of the mortise. Then cut in from the side to form the cheeks.

The hole for the pin—a dowel of approximately $\frac{1}{2}$ in. *(12 mm)* is drilled through the sides of the mortise before the tenon is set in place. When the hole is drilled, insert the tenon into the mortise and tap in until the cheeks of the tenon part are tight to the mortise part.

Push your drill into the hole to mark the center of the hole on the tenon part, withdraw the tenon and drill the hole about $\frac{1}{16}$ in. *(1.5 mm)* away from the end of the piece of wood. Thus, when the pin is driven into the tenon through the mortise it will draw the cheeks firmly in place.

If your tenon sticks through the mortise, simply trim it off. Likewise trim the dowel flush.

Mortise and tenon joints should always be glued.

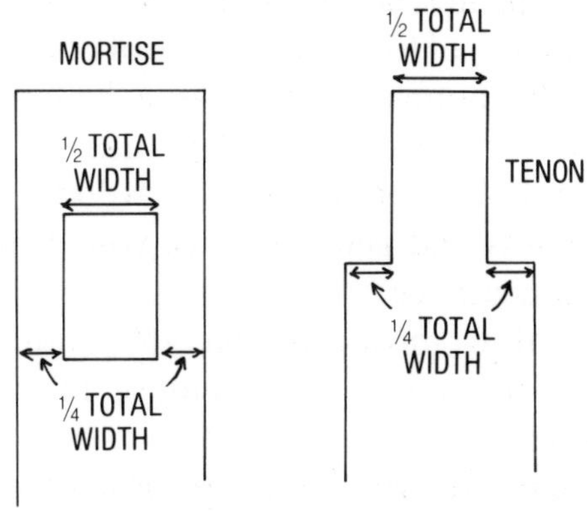

Mortise and Tenon Joint No. 1

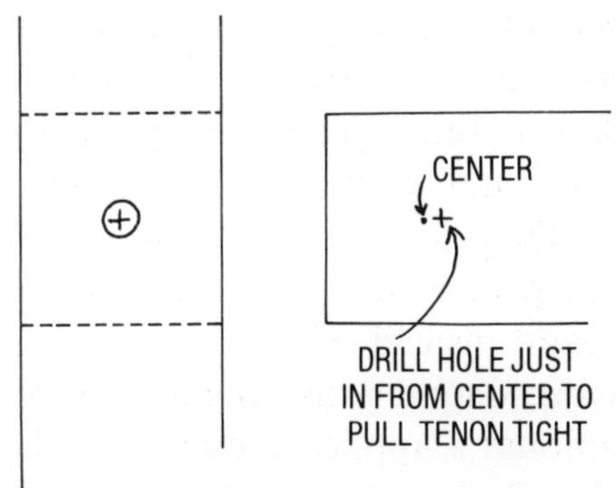

Mortise and Tenon Joint No. 2

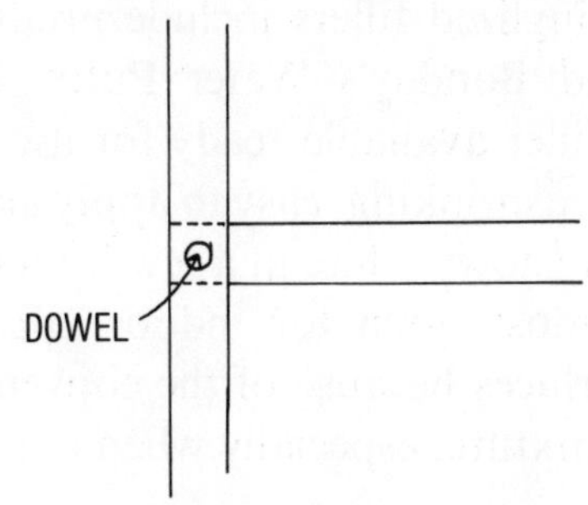

Mortise and Tenon Joint No. 3

DOWELS

The designs in this book require the use of a lot of dowels. The holes for the dowels must closely match the diameter of the dowels. Dowels are not made to precise sizes; also, wood expands and contracts according to its moisture content. Thus, the diameter of the dowel depends to a certain degree on the moisture content of the wood when the dowel was cut and the moisture content when you use it.

When making holes for dowels I generally use the flat wood-boring bits for an electric drill. Because these drill bits are not accurately cut, either, I modify my bits to suit the size of the dowel. The dowels are often undersized, so when making a hole for a $\frac{1}{2}$ in. *(12 mm)* dowel, I first make a test hole with my $\frac{1}{2}$ in. *(12 mm)* bit to test the dowel diameter. The hole is usually too big, but the problem can be corrected by filing off some of the drill bit.

This is most easily done with the bit in the drill, the drill held firmly on your lap, and the file in your right hand. Before starting to file, look closely at the bit and you will notice that the edges are beveled in one direction. Maintain that bevel while filing and file off the same amount on each side edge of the bit.

You need not take off very much: a dozen strokes the length of the cutting edge on both edges is probably enough. Make another test hole and file off some more if necessary.

Because flat wood-boring bits are cheap and are not highly tempered, they are relatively soft. If you have a good, highly tempered set you may have problems filing the steel.

When drilling holes for doweling of $\frac{3}{4}$ in. *(20 mm)* diameter or larger, I use an expansive bit. I also use an expansive bit with my carpenter's brace because it is more manageable than an electric drill and bit when drilling large-diameter holes.

WOOD FILLERS

Every carpenter needs to use some kind of wood filler. The use of filler is not a sign of poor carpentry; rather, the nonuse of filler is a hallmark of the inexperienced carpenter. Wood filler will fill in nail or screw holes and voids in plywood, tidy up ill-fitting joints and generally give your handiwork a neater appearance.

The three most common types of fillers are the plastic wood types, the cellulose fillers and the vinylized fillers.

The plastic wood fillers are best when you want a natural wood finish, since they can be purchased in different shades or stained to match light or dark woods. When varnished over they are hardly noticeable. Of the three, these fillers are the most expensive and most difficult to work with.

Cellulose fillers such as Polyfilla are good for general use and work well on wood, plaster or masonry. They come in the form of a powder and are mixed with water; for water resistance use an enamel paint instead of water. Cellulose fillers are inexpensive, simple to use and do not shrink unless a large amount is applied at one time. They dry into a grayish color and are easily sanded because of their plaster-like texture.

The vinylized fillers include products such as Polyfix and Bondex's Water Putty. Polyfix is a premixed filler available ready for use in a tube or can. It is nonshrinking, easy to apply and sand, and dries into a snowy white in a few hours' time. I use this filler most often for indoor applications on painted surfaces because of the convenience of the prepared mixture, especially when only a little dab is required.

The many fillers on the market all have advantages and disadvantages for various applications. Ask your store clerk for advice.

Wood fillers are best applied with a putty knife and can be smoothed with ordinary sandpaper.

SCREWS

When setting flat-head wood screws through one piece of wood to thread into another piece of wood, you must make three holes to hold the pieces together. The pilot hole is the first and the smallest in diameter. This is the guide hole that the threads of the screw will follow. It must be smaller than the diameter of the threads of the screw size you are using. It is also drilled first through both pieces of wood that are to be joined.

The second hole to make is the shank hole, which should be just larger than the smooth shank of the screw and follows the pilot hole through only the first piece of wood.

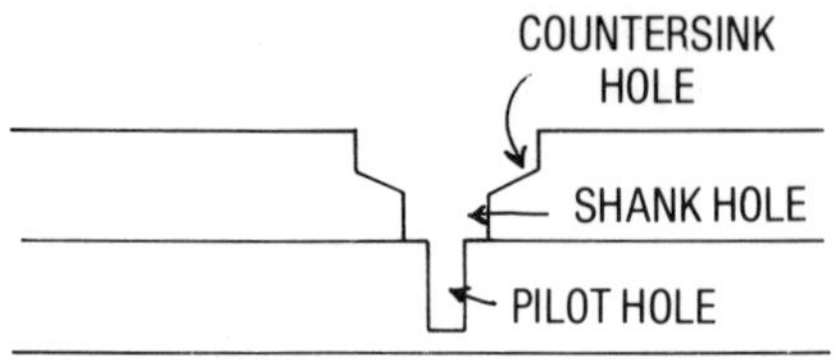

The third hole is the countersink hole. It accommodates the head of the screw, which is recessed below the surface of the wood, and should be just larger than the screw head.

All three holes can be made at once using combination countersink drill bits, which come in different sizes for the various screw sizes. Or you can drill the holes separately, changing bits for each hole. This method can be tedious if a large number of screws must be set, but for the projects in this book, it is practical since most pieces require only a few screws.

FINISHING

Under this heading I include: smoothing—planing rough spots and edges, rounding corners and general preparation for filling and sanding; filling—the use of wood fillers; sanding—the sanding smooth of wood and fillers; and painting or varnishing.

Infants, toddlers and preschoolers are always crawling and falling into the most unlikely places. They must be protected from sharp corners, protruding bolt ends and hard edges. You cannot protect children from everything that might injure them, but you can reduce the possibility of mishaps.

SMOOTHING

When constructing furniture I watch out for rough spots. I keep my block plane handy to smooth the edges of boards and to take off the splinters from saw cuts. A few quick strokes along the lower edge of the board where the saw has just cut can make a world of difference. Any edges that will be exposed when the piece is finished also get a stroke of the plane to take off the sharp corners.

I almost always round off exposed corners. This can be done with a Surform file or by cutting on a radius with a coping saw or saber saw. The larger the piece, the larger the rounding radius. I rarely mark the corners with a compass, but instead use anything round that is handy: bottoms of paint tins, bowls, beer bottles. I have no rule of thumb to go by; I simply decide what is a pleasant curve as I look at it. With a bit of experience and some confidence, the rounding is quickly done.

FILLING

Since I have already discussed the choices of wood fillers, this section deals with only the procedure of filling. I apply wood filler before sanding, thereby greatly reducing the amount of sanding required. I apply the filler with a putty knife and allow it to dry for the prescribed time. I then sand the filled spots, adding more filler if needed before sanding the whole piece. I try to ensure that all rough spots, indentations from hammer blows, and nail-head holes have been filled. When working with finishing nails I use a small nail punch to tap the nail head just below the surface of the wood, making the nail invisible after the hole has been filled.

When using wood filler, try to apply it as smoothly as possible. This not only saves on sanding, but also reduces the amount of dust flying around while preparing for painting.

When using plywood, I generally apply wood filler on all the exposed edges. Plywood, with its laminations, does not give a smooth edge when painted over. By using the filler generously you can substantially improve the look of your new piece.

SANDING

After all holes and voids have been filled and the filler is dry, begin sanding. Use a medium or fine paper on the filler because a coarse paper will deeply score it. Sand the filled places smooth, then thoroughly sand the whole piece with a medium-grit paper.

Sandpaper comes in a variety of grits and grades, the three most common types being the flint papers, garnet papers and aluminum oxide papers. Flint paper is the cheapest and wears out the fastest, while garnet and aluminum oxide papers last and remain sharp longer, but are more expensive.

It might sound odd to say that sandpaper remains sharp, but the particles stuck to the paper backing must be sharp to maintain their cutting ability. Garnet paper and especially aluminum oxide paper become clogged up or torn before they wear out. To make the paper last longer I clean it off with a wire brush when it becomes clogged with sawdust.

As the sandpaper gets duller it may no longer be up to its proper grit. When the bite has gone out of a piece of coarse paper, I use it as medium paper. The same goes for slightly clogged and worn medium paper, which becomes fine paper. When sanding between coats of paint or varnish I use old pieces of sandpaper, since the paper quickly becomes clogged and then is useless.

When varnishing a piece and giving it the five or six coats recommended for a deep and tough finish, I try to use the same piece of fine paper between each coat. With the sanding between each coat the paper becomes more clogged and dull. By the final coat it hardly roughs the varnished surface and gives a smooth finish.

I use a satin varnish because if some rough particles have dried in it, I can touch up the piece after the final coat with that old piece of sandpaper.

As well, some extrafine paper (220 grit) is handy to have for light touch-up jobs. I buy coarse aluminum oxide paper, garnet medium and flint fine paper.

The coarse paper should be used only on the end grain and saw cuts. Medium paper is used for general sanding on all surfaces and for any areas that have been sanded with coarse paper. Fine paper is used over everything just before painting.

Always sand the undercoat. With softwood—especially the poplar plywood, which seems to have a peach fuzz on its surface—no matter how much sanding I do before painting or varnishing, the undercoat is rough when dry. I sand off most of the undercoat and then give the piece a second application of undercoat. By the time I've finished sanding the second undercoat, the piece is baby smooth and the top coat just glides on to cover the wood well.

When sanding it is much easier to use a sanding block with the sandpaper wrapped around it. I make a block from a 5 in. *(130 mm)* piece of 2 in. x 2 in. *(38 mm x 38 mm)* and wrap it in four or five layers of soft cloth such as a couple of old socks folded back and forth over the block surface. I then tear a sheet of sandpaper in two, wrap it around the cloth-covered block, grip it with my hand, and sand. The cloth cushions the sandpaper so that it forms itself to the surface of the wood being sanded rather than to the block itself.

PAINTING OR VARNISHING

I have discussed the choice of paints and finishes in an earlier section; this section covers only the procedure of painting.

A good paintbrush is the most important tool for applying the finishing coats. A high-quality brush produces a smooth finish whereas a poor-quality brush gives poor covering and a streaky finish. It is tempting to pick up an inexpensive brush and assume it will suffice. It will do the job, but not a good job. As a general rule, the smoother and softer the brush, the smoother and more even the finish.

When at the store, pick out a cheap brush, then the most expensive brush. Run both brushes over your hand and you can feel the difference. With the cheap brush you will constantly be picking hairs out of the paint and will have to go over the surface of your piece several times to get the same quality finish as with the good brush.

With proper care, a good brush can last for years. The low-quality brush will probably be discarded after a few uses because it sheds hair like an angora cat in summer.

Instead of cleaning my brushes after every use, I store them in a large can, such as a paint tin, with a small amount of solvent in the bottom. I use a large can (a one gallon paint can) so that the lid can be put on tightly with the brushes inside.

While painting and varnishing I keep a varnish brush in one can and a paintbrush in another. When a brush is needed I simply swish it around a bit in the solvent, wipe off the excess solvent on the can rim, then shake out any remaining solvent.

After several uses a sludge of paint will build up at the bottom of the can. Let the sediment settle, then pour off the clear solvent. Dump out the sludge and remaining solvent and clean the can. Pour the cleaner solvent back into the can, add more solvent and keep using it. Thus you use a relatively small amount of solvent and your brushes are always ready for use. I do not leave my brushes like this in a can of solvent for long periods of time. Two weeks, even if they are used frequently, is about maximum.

If you will not be using your brushes for a long time, clean them thoroughly with several rinsings of solvent. Save the solvent in which you rinsed the brush in the can for future use.

You will note that the undercoat of paint or the first coat of varnish quickly soaks into the wood, resulting in a coat that's streaky and thin. This is because the undercoat of paint is meant to be both a sealer and a filler—to seal the surface of the wood and to fill the pores and grain of the wood. Sanding down the undercoat can be thought of as reducing the wood surface to the lowest common level, which is then built up to the desired depth of finish.

No special care is needed for the first undercoat, although it should be applied evenly. The top coat should be brushed all in the same direction for a really smooth finish. Dip your brush lightly into the paint; remove any excess that may drip from the brush by wiping the brush on the rim; then apply with a smooth, even stroke along the grain of the wood. Avoid brushing back and forth, which tends to make the top coat uneven.

If a hair comes off the brush or you notice a bit of sawdust or other imperfection on the freshly painted surface, pick it off with a cloth or your fingernail. Smooth the area over with a few strokes of the brush.

My painted surfaces usually have three coats: two undercoats and one top coat. The varnished surfaces get five or six coats of urethane varnish for indoor finishes, or three or four coats of an exterior varnish for outdoor finishes.

Projects that remain outside, such as the outdoor gym, or toys that get a lot of abuse, such as the stilts, are best given an oil-based stain. This finish is a wood preservative and soaks into the wood. It will not chip and flake off with heavy use as do paint and varnish.

Oil-based stain finishes need periodic renewal, since the surface weathers and fades. Brush one or two coats on new wood and renew annually.

Metrics

Although the pieces in this book were all built using imperial-sized wood, tools and fastenings, metric equivalents have been included. The dimensions given, however, may not correspond exactly to what will be available when all lumber, tools and fastenings are sold in metric sizes.

I used the lumber dimensions published in the Metric Handbook for Canadian Softwood Lumber, compiled by Metric Sub-sector Committee 8.21—Softwood Lumber for Metric Commission Canada, November 1977.

As any experienced woodworker knows, finished lumber is not the size of its nominal name. A 1 in. x 2 in. is finished green at ¾ in. x 1⁹⁄₁₆ in. Its dry size is ¹¹⁄₁₆ in. x 1½ in. The Metric Handbook states that the equivalent dry size of the metric counterpart of a 1 in. x 2 in. is *17 mm x 38 mm.*

No one from the Metric Commission could tell me if the lumberyards will list the 1 in. x 2 in. metric equivalent as *25 mm x 50 mm* (the rough conversion of 1 in. x 2 in.) or *17 mm x 38 mm.*

Likewise, the size of plywood sheets will be changed. The thickness will be given in millimeters, but the overall size of the sheet will be smaller. A sheet of metric plywood will be *1200 mm x 2400 mm.* This is 1½ in. *(38 mm)* shorter and ¾ in. *(19 mm)* narrower than the present 4 ft. x 8 ft. plywood sheet.

When I give metric dimensions for plywood layouts, I have taken into account the smaller metric sheet of plywood. Thus the same project, such as the indoor gym or toy box, will be slightly smaller so that it can be cut from the metric sheet of plywood.

Another difficulty in metric conversion seems to fall at the ¾ in. *(19 mm)* mark. The metric equivalent of ¾ in. drill sizes, plywood thickness, screw or nail length, and dowel diameter may appear in this book as *18 mm, 19 mm* or *20 mm* depending on the use of the aforementioned articles.

Every effort has been made to ensure that the reader can use either measurements—metric or imperial.

Wood

I generally use standard construction-grade wood to make furniture. There may be some knots that have to be cut out, or some warped portions of boards that must be cut into short pieces to be usable, but construction grades are adequate for most projects. The cost difference between them and select or clear grades is so great that it is still cheaper to allow for some waste with the lower-grade wood when necessary. Select grades are often as much as twice the cost of construction grades.

I use pine or fir for nearly everything. Pine is softer and slightly easier to work with; however, because of its softness, it dents easily with heavy use. Fir is harder and stronger but more prone to splitting, and in some areas it may be more expensive.

Cedar is excellent for outdoor use because it is more rot resistant than pine or fir. It is more brittle and in the 1 in. *(17 mm)* thickness splits easily when nailed. It has about the same dent resistance, or hardness, as pine and is also good for general-purpose use.

Spruce is acceptable for general use, being stronger than pine, but a smooth finish is harder to achieve on this type of wood. It tends to have more knots with a swirling grain that cannot easily be sanded or planed smooth, and it is also the least attractive of the above-mentioned woods. Spruce is inexpensive and readily available, since it is commonly used for studs, sheathing and strapping in house construction.

When selecting wood, look over every piece carefully for loose knots that might fall out. Also, do not accept a board that has a knot across most of its width, for the knot will greatly weaken the wood and will have to be cut out.

WARPING

Another defect to look for is warping in its various forms. A wide board or plank may have a cupping warp across its width. Fir tends to twist along its length with a corkscrew-type bending, and so does spruce. It is easy to check for warping by laying the piece on a flat surface and looking to see whether one corner is lifting off the surface. If the board is to be cut in shorter pieces, the warp will partially disappear, but this type of warping is the most difficult to deal with.

Bowing is also a common form of warping, with a hump or dip in the middle of the length of the piece. Again if the wood is to be cut in shorter pieces, the warp may be eliminated. With wood that is still damp or green, a weight placed at the point of greatest bow will sometimes gradually straighten the board over a period of a few weeks.

DRYNESS

Some woods are kiln-dried at the mill, meaning that they are placed in a huge ovenlike affair and cooked dry to reach a low moisture content. This method of drying is faster than air drying, but when the wood arrives at your door it may not be at the same moisture content as when it left the mill. It may have been left outside in the rain and snow to soak up moisture. Even when damp, kiln-dried wood will be drier than green wood, since the natural moisture (sap or pitch) has been dried out of it; but it will have to be dried in your workshop before being used.

Air dry damp wood by stacking it up with some scrap pieces between each of the boards. Be sure the surface is flat and the scrap pieces are all the same thickness, or the wood may dry to a warped shape. A week or two of storing the boards in a warm, dry environment should rid them of soaked-up moisture.

Wood that is not kiln-dried is said to be air-dried. Properly, the wood should be stacked up with strips between boards every 3 ft. to 4 ft. *(900 mm to 1200 mm).* In practice, it is usually sawed, stacked on pallets and bound together with steel strapping for shipment. It then travels overland, most often by train, to arrive at the local lumberyard, where it is sold usually straight from the bound-up bundles. Even though it may have been months in transit, the wood is still green and contains a lot of natural moisture.

This non-kiln-dried wood will have to be dried after you buy it. It will be damp and sticky to touch and will shred when planed or sanded. If the wood is varnished or painted before it is dry, the moisture will eventually lift the finish and make it tacky.

As an example of this, I recently bought twelve pieces of cedar 1 in. x 6 in. *(17 mm x 140 mm).* I stacked the wood in the basement a short distance away from the furnace, and it was two months before I could work with it properly.

If I have only a few small pieces such as 1 in. x 2 in. *(17 mm x 38 mm)* or 2 in. x 2 in. *(38 mm x 38 mm)*, I hang some wire coat hangers on nails running along the floor joists in the basement about 24 in. *(600 mm)* apart. I then lay the pieces on the inside of the hangers and suspend them in the air. The wood should be ready for use in a couple of weeks. (Be sure not to hang it where water pipes could drip on it.)

PLYWOOD

I generally use fir "good one side" (GIS) plywood for most projects. It is easily worked, inexpensive, readily available and very durable. On the "non-good" side it will have some voids which can be filled with wood filler for a painted finish. Once filled and painted, the voids will not be noticeable if on the underside or inside of your furniture.

Plywood with both sides good is also available, although slightly more expensive. I buy poplar plywood when I want both sides good, since this is the least expensive plywood in my area.

Particle board—also known as plate board, pressboard or chipboard—can sometimes be substituted for plywood. Particle board is made of wood chips saturated with glue, then rolled into sheets the same dimensions as plywood. It is especially attractive when various hardwood veneers are laid over the chip surface. I often buy birch veneer particle board.

Although particle board is less expensive than plywood, it cannot always substitute for it. Plate board tends to delaminate and warp when wet. It does not hold nails or screws as well as plywood, especially nails or screws in the edges.

Veneer taping can be applied with contact cement to the particle board edges, giving the appearance of solid wood. When the board is trimmed, sanded and varnished, the effect is very attractive.

Particle board could be used instead of plywood for the first cradle, the toy box and the indoor gym, but only if the indoor gym always stays indoors.

DOWELS

Many of the projects I show in the book use dowels as a major part of their construction. For most of the pieces I specify softwood dowels bought in random lengths, which is by far the cheapest way to buy dowels, although not all lumberyards carry them. By calling around I located a yard where I could buy these dowels in lengths from 6 ft. to 14 ft. *(2 m to 4 m)*, and from ½ in. to 1½ in. *(12 mm to 38 mm)* in diameter. Many lumberyards carry only the hardwood dowels in 3 ft. or 4 ft. *(1 m or 1.4 m)* lengths. The softwood dowels generally cost about one-third the price of the shorter lengths of hardwood dowels.

When buying softwood dowels, add up the various lengths and order longer pieces. For example, for the first cradle you need 30 in. *(650 mm)* pieces of dowel ¾ in. *(18 mm)* in diameter. A 10 ft.

(*3 m*) length yields four pieces with no waste.

It is best to use a miter box to cut dowels, since making a square cut on a round piece of wood is difficult when cutting to length by hand. The miter box is also handy for cutting $\frac{3}{4}$ in. x $\frac{3}{4}$ in. (*17 mm x 17 mm*) or quarter round.

QUARTER ROUND

On most of the designs, quarter round and $\frac{3}{4}$ in. x $\frac{3}{4}$ in. (*17 mm x 17 mm*) are interchangeable. There is little difference in cost. The quarter round gives a nice smooth side. Also, you may have some scrap quarter round in the house left over from molding around the baseboards. I often use old quarter round; if the old paint is sanded and the nail holes filled, it can be very serviceable.

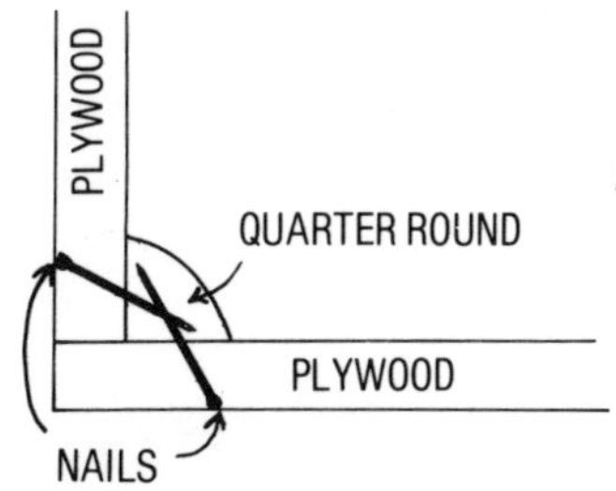

Nailing into Quarter Round

The only caution in using quarter round is that when nailing into it through plywood you must be sure that the nail goes into the thickest part. (See illustration.) If your nail point does break through the surface, either pound it back out and set the nail again or, if only the tip is sticking through, just file it off. Do not try to crimp the nail points over; you will make a mess of the wood and the nail will be loosened.

Tools

HANDSAWS

Crosscut

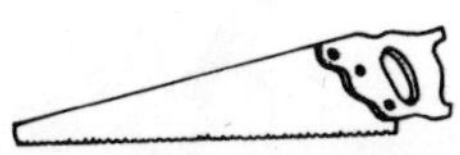

An 8-point (8 teeth per 1 in./25 mm) crosscut saw with a 26 in. (*660 mm*) blade, is fine for general use. A Teflon-coated blade is a good choice since it does not stick in resinous woods, and the Teflon prevents the blade from getting rusty.

Panel Saw

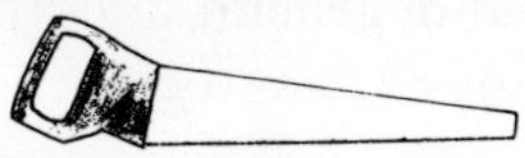

A 22 in. (*560 mm*) blade, 12 point, is good for cutting plywood and other thin woods. It leaves a cleaner cut than the crosscut saw, but is slower in cutting. The panel saw can be used instead of the crosscut saw for the articles in this book.

Backsaw or Miter Saw

Usually with 14 in. or 16 in. (*360 mm or 400 mm*) blade and 10 or 12 point, this saw is meant for use with a miter box. It is also good for making fine and accurate cuts as in mortise and tenon joints (required only for the baby crib).

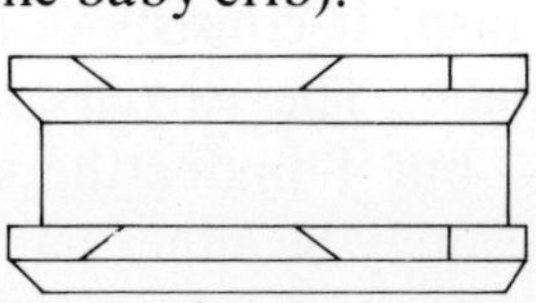

Miter Box

The miter box is used with the backsaw or miter saw to cut small pieces of wood, either straight cuts or at a 45° angle. One of the small wooden miter boxes is adequate for our purposes.

Coping Saw

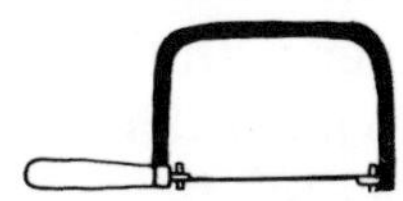

The coping saw comes with a 6 in. (*150 mm*) removable blade. Use medium or fine blades. This saw is intended for rounding corners or making any curved cuts. It does most things an electric saber saw can do.

Compass or Keyhole Saw

The compass or keyhole saw starts cuts from a drilled hole and can make gently curving cuts.

Electric Saws

Saber Saw or Jigsaw

This saw makes curved cuts, can start a cut from a drilled hole and replaces the compass and coping saws. It is a good item for the type of projects found in this book. I have a light-duty two-speed saber saw.

Circular Saw

The circular saw makes straight cuts and can crosscut or rip with various blades. It replaces the crosscut handsaw but is not necessary for small projects such as in this book.

HAND DRILLS

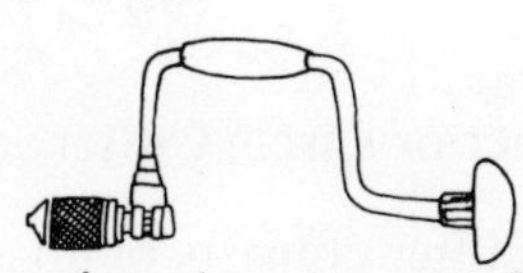

Carpenter's Brace

The carpenter's brace is a handy tool for drilling holes of $\frac{1}{4}$ in. (*6 mm*) diameter and larger. It is especially useful for making holes of $\frac{3}{4}$ in. (*18 mm*) diameter or larger with an expansive bit. Only square-shanked auger bits can be used with this drill, not the flat wood-boring bits.

Hand Drill, Pinion Type

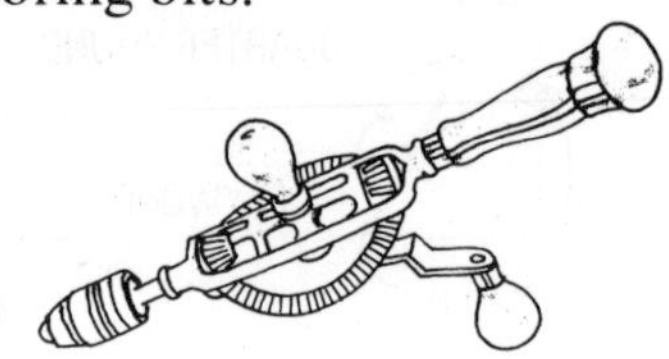

This drill is useful for making holes of $\frac{1}{4}$ in. *(6 mm)* diameter and smaller, such as screw pilot holes. A double-pinion drill is better and lasts longer than the single-pinion type.

Electric Drill

I have a $\frac{1}{4}$ in. *(6 mm)* electric drill and consider it my handiest shop tool. It drills holes of all sizes: up to $\frac{1}{4}$ in. *(6 mm)* diameter with twist-drill bits; $\frac{3}{8}$ in. to 1 in. *(10 mm to 25 mm)* diameter with flat wood-boring bits; 1 in. to $2\frac{1}{2}$ in. *(25 mm to 63 mm)* diameter with a hole-saw set; and holes up to 4 in. *(100 mm)* diameter with a wing cutter. The latter two tools are also used for making wheels.

Flat Wood-Boring Bits

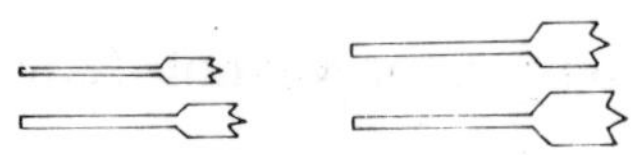

These come in sets with sizes of $\frac{3}{8}$ in. to 1 in. *(10 mm to 25 mm)*, and are useful for drilling holes for dowels.

Hole-Saw Set

The hole-saw set consists of a set of saw-toothed metal rings that mount on a drill arbor. By removing the unwanted sizes you can cut a perfect circle or wheel from 1 in. to $2\frac{1}{2}$ in. *(25 mm to 63 mm)* in diameter.

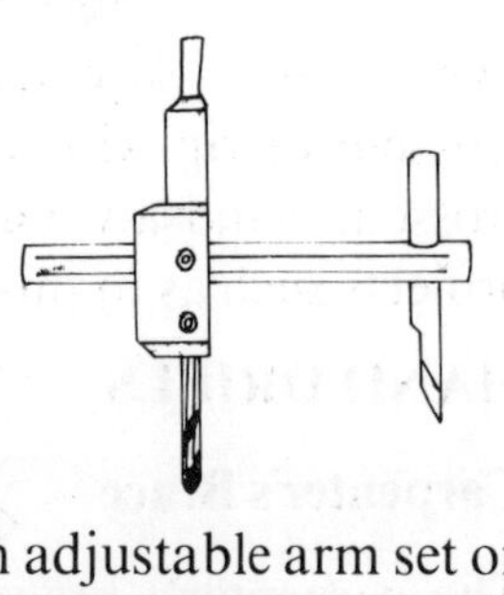

Wing Cutter or Circle Cutter

The wing cutter consists of an adjustable arm set on a drill mount to cut holes of larger diameter. It will cut wheels if the cutter or the drill is reversed.

Combination Countersink Drill Bits

These drill bits are for setting screws. They drill the countersink hole, the shank hole and the pilot hole for the screw all at the same time. They are handy when setting a large number of flat-head wood screws.

SQUARES

Carpenter's Square

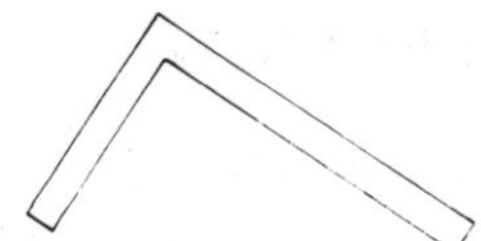

This item is a 24 in. x 16 in. *(610 mm x 400 mm)* metal square. It is indispensable for marking straight cuts, checking corners and laying out plywood sheets for cutting.

Combination Square

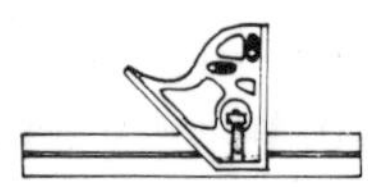

This square has a 12 in. *(300 mm)* sliding/locking metal rule mounted on a carrier that incorporates a level and a 45° angle. It is handy for marking small items, checking corners and ensuring straight cuts.

PLANES

Block or Jack Plane

The block and jack are actually two different types of planes, but are very similar. The jack plane is slightly larger and more heavily built, has more adjustments and is more expensive. They both do the same job—that of general smoothing, rounding edges and removing excess stock.

Spokeshave

This is an inexpensive type of plane that is good for general smoothing and rounding edges. It was originally used for making rounded spokes for wagon wheels. When using the spokeshave, care should be taken to see that you do not create a wavy surface because of the short carriage.

SURFORM FILE

This is a modified type of wood rasp but much more useful than a rasp. It consists of a carrier with a replacement blade. The carriers come in several different types, but I prefer the straight-handled type. The blades may be either flat or rounded: the rounded blades are best because they cut more efficiently than the flat type. This tool is used for rounding edges and corners, forming shapes and removing excess stock.

HAMMER 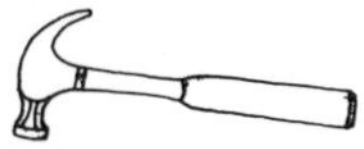

The standard claw hammer has a 16 oz. *(450 g)* head. For building the furniture in this book, a 12 oz. *(300 g)* head would be better. I like a wood handle, but many people break these handles when pulling nails, and prefer a steel-shank hammer.

SCREWDRIVERS 

Screwdrivers come in a multitude of shapes and sizes. A flat blade for slot-headed screws and a Robertson head for socket-type screws are most common. Obtain the size screwdriver for the size of screws you are using.

NAIL PUNCH 

A small punch about 3 in. to 4 in. *(75 mm to 100 mm)* long is useful for tapping the heads of finishing nails below the surface of the wood. It eliminates dents in the wood from hammer blows.

WOOD CHISEL 

A good-quality chisel of ½ in. *(12 mm)*—the width of the cutting edge—will see you through most jobs. A chisel is necessary for making mortise and tenon joints, and cross-lap joints.

MEASURING TAPE 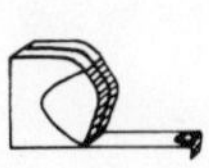

A 10 ft. *(3 m)* steel tape is a good choice.

CHOOSING NECESSARY TOOLS

Deciding what is necessary in the way of tools depends very much on your budget, strength and ability. For instance, you could do a very good job constructing the projects in this book with only hand tools. It would take more time and effort, but the tools would cost less than the electric tools to do the same job.

You could also go to the other extreme by purchasing all electric tools of good quality, thereby spending large sums of money to equip your workshop.

I use only two electric tools: a ¼ in. *(6 mm)* drill and a saber saw. Hand tools are adequate for all other tasks.

I list below the tools recommended for undertaking the projects in this book. This would be a good beginner's list for someone who plans to build several of the pieces and then go on to further woodworking projects. More tools can be added as required.

26 in. *(660 mm)* crosscut saw
16 in. *(400 mm)* miter saw and miter box
saber saw (electric)
¼ in. *(6 mm)* electric drill
set of flat wood-boring bits
set of twist drills up to ¼ in. *(6 mm)* diameter
hole-saw set
16 oz. *(450 g)* claw hammer
8 in. *(200 mm)* block plane
carpenter's square
½ in. *(12 mm)* wood chisel
10 ft. *(3 m)* steel tape
flat file
various screwdrivers

With careful shopping, the cost of the above list can be kept within reason, but do not buy the cheapest model available of all the tools. Get a good crosscut saw because this will be the most used tool. Buy a good-quality drill and saber saw while scrimping on the other tools as your budget dictates.

If you already own or can borrow some tools, you are steps ahead of the cost.

When Christmas is coming up, or a birthday, you could show the above list to someone who is buying you a present. A carpenter's square might not be the most elegant gift under the Christmas tree, but it will be greatly appreciated in the workshop.

If you have no tools and do not want to invest in any before trying your hand at woodworking, consider signing up for evening woodworking classes at your local secondary school or community center. At the classes you will need some projects; show this book to the instructor and I am sure you can agree on a few of the articles.

At the introduction to each project I list the tools necessary for its construction. Choose a project that requires only a few tools and try your hand. If you enjoy the work, you can acquire the tools for other projects as you go along.

An example of the simplest project would be the crib faces, which can be made with only a coping saw and drill. I built the first cradle with only a handsaw, coping saw, drill and square.